TRAITOR

BY

DEFAULT

TRAITOR

BY

DEFAULT

The Trials of Kanao Inouye,
the Kamloops Kid

PATRICK BRODE

DUNDURN
PRESS

Publisher: Meghan Macdonald | Editor: Robyn So
Cover designer: Karen Alexiou
Cover image: Kanao Inouye in British custody, c. 1946–47. George B. Puddicombe fonds, Library and Archives Canada, 3816977; barbed wire: ILYA AKINSHIN/shutterstock.com

Library and Archives Canada Cataloguing in Publication

Title: Traitor by default : the trials of Kanao Inouye, the Kamloops Kid / Patrick Brode.
Names: Brode, Patrick, 1950- author.
Description: Includes bibliographical references and index.
Identifiers: Canadiana (print) 20230622828 | Canadiana (ebook) 20230623115 | ISBN 9781459753693 (softcover) | ISBN 9781459753709 (PDF) | ISBN 9781459753716 (EPUB)
Subjects: LCSH: Inouye, Kanao—Trials, litigation, etc. | LCSH: War crime trials—China— Hong Kong—History—20th century. | LCSH: World War, 1939-1945—Atrocities—Japan. | LCSH: World War, 1939-1945—Atrocities—China—Hong Kong. | CSH: Japanese Canadians—Biography.
Classification: LCC KZ1186.I56 B76 2024 | DDC 341.6/9026841052—dc23

We acknowledge the support of the Canada Council for the Arts and the Ontario Arts Council for our publishing program. We also acknowledge the financial support of the Government of Ontario, through the Ontario Book Publishing Tax Credit and Ontario Creates, and the Government of Canada.

Dundurn Press
1382 Queen Street East
Toronto, Ontario, Canada M4L 1C9
dundurn.com, @dundurnpress

CONTENTS

Introduction 1

1 Arrival 5

2 Sham Shui Po 17

3 Kempeitai 25

4 Arrest 35

5 Political Football 47

6 Godown Justice 55

7 Only Obeying Orders 71

8 Decision Annulled 87

9 Treason? 99

10 Defence Gamble 111

11 Exhibit C 121

12 Technicalities of Law 135

13 End of a Scruffy Show 145

Acknowledgements 159

Appendix 161

Notes 163

Image Credits 183

Index 185

About the Author 191

INTRODUCTION

STANLEY PRISON, HONG KONG: 7:00 A.M., August 26, 1947

THE PRISONER SHOWED LITTLE EMOTION WHEN THE EXECUTION PARTY arrived in his cell first thing that morning. He was thirty-one years old and very thin after almost two years of imprisonment. The prison staff undoubtedly had figured in his diminished weight in calculating the appropriate drop to achieve a sudden and decorous death. They had hanged people before.

The man they were about to hang had lived an eventful life. In fact, he left several life stories behind him, each one contradicting the others. To the end, the determination of who he was and where his loyalties lay was a profound mystery. That he had been born in Kamloops, British Columbia, was one of few facts that was beyond dispute. But his conduct during the war was a mass of conflicting stories. There was one other fact about him that remained without question. He had been convicted by a Hong Kong court of treason to the British Crown and would hang for it.

Only a few days before his scheduled execution he wrote to King George VI in the hope that there would be clemency. Referring to himself repeatedly as "your humble petitioner," he begged the King to consider that despite his

Canadian birth he was a devoted Japanese subject and that it was only due to "my ignorance of the technicalities of law of changing nationality" that he was left in his current predicament. It was a vain hope, and it seemed unlikely that the petition would even arrive in Britain before his sentence was carried out.

This particular execution would be one of the last acts of the recent war. In fact, it was almost an afterthought; the press would pay little attention to it. Life in Hong Kong had moved on and the government was preparing celebrations to mark the second anniversary of the end of the Japanese occupation. In Canada, the hanging passed without much comment even though it was only the second time in history that a Canadian faced execution for treason. Ottawa officials had always been uneasy about the case, for it raised too many questions that reflected on the government's internment of the Japanese minority during the war and the deportation of hundreds of others afterward. It was a major relief when British colonial authorities assumed control.

After all, getting on with life was far more important in Canada. Back in the condemned man's hometown of Kamloops, veterans had all long ago been welcomed home at formal parades. After the speeches and applause faded, they braced themselves for the race for jobs. Even the condemned man's family back in Canada had not heard from him in many years. One group that did remember him was a small cadre of Canadian Hong Kong veterans. Many of them recalled how quick he had been to slap and humiliate them. To his Canadian victims, the "Kamloops Kid" had arrived at a well-deserved ending.

Though his execution was largely ignored at the time, over the years his story would be revived, embellished, and distorted beyond recognition. In following decades, he would become the embodiment of evil, a sadist who well deserved the ignominy of hanging. All too often, these tales would be based on rumour and innuendo and without any appreciation of the facts or the context of his situation. The central question of whether he was Japanese or Canadian would all but be forgotten.

All the ferment of the post-war world meant nothing to the young man in the death cell who, in a few moments, would face execution. We have little idea what thoughts occupied his mind in these final minutes. Perhaps he had flashes of the wife and child outside of Stanley Prison who he would never see again. Now, his only option was to manage the style of his death. Should he die quietly as a convicted criminal, or should he make a dramatic gesture to his homeland? In either case, it was apparent that the years that might have stretched before him were about to end in a sudden, violent strangulation. It was an unforeseen outcome to an extraordinary series of events.

1

ARRIVAL

HE WAS THE SON OF A HERO.

During the First World War, Kanao Inouye's[1] father served in the Canadian Expeditionary Force (CEF). A tough, valiant soldier, he was one of many men who established the CEF's reputation as a formidable army and a source of national pride. Even before the war, the elder Inouye had shown the resilience to adapt and prosper in his adopted land. It had not been an easy, or a welcoming, prospect.

Tadashi — or "Tow" as he became known in Canada — Inouye was born in Yokohama, Kanagawa Prefecture, Japan, on October 16, 1883, and came to Canada in 1905. Over five thousand Japanese emigrants entered the country between 1898 and 1900, and almost all of them came to Canada's westernmost province, British Columbia.[2] Prior to 1898, the British Columbia government had done what it could to restrict Japanese immigration, and those who did enter were disenfranchised and could not expect to get citizenship rights. While the Royal Commission on Chinese and Japanese Immigration, Session 1902, reported that the Japanese were "less undesirable than the Chinese," it concluded that "they [the Japanese] are quite as serious a menace as the Chinese."[3] There were persistent fears that the hardworking Japanese would supplant white labour, and after 1900, the B.C. government announced that it would enact laws to formally stop any more Japanese from entering the province. This was forestalled by a "gentleman's agreement"[4] whereby Japan voluntarily agreed to ban further immigration to Canada. The agreement effectively curtailed emigration from Japan until 1905, when the pace again picked up and new arrivals such as Tow Inouye entered the country. Nativist agitation soon followed, and in 1907, the Asiatic Exclusion League was formed. An anti-Asian race riot that year in Vancouver caught the government's attention, and in late 1907, Sir Wilfrid Laurier, the prime minister, recognized the need to appease the province and British Columbians' fear of "a quiet, persistent and systematic Japanese invasion."[5]

Many young Japanese men like Tow Inouye arrived eagerly, believing in the propaganda of emigration agents that "America" — usually inclusive of Canada — was a golden land where fortunes could be made. The regulations required Japanese emigrants to return to their native country in three years, but the rules were not rigorously enforced, and permanent emigration became the reality. In some ways, Canada was indeed a land of opportunity. Those who fished at the mouth of the Fraser River found that if they worked hard enough, a living could be had. By 1900, almost two thousand Japanese worked the fisheries on B.C.'s West Coast. Others worked in the coal mines. Other major sources of employment were lumber camps and pulp and paper mills of the Interior. Work gangs of Japanese labourers usually worked separately from whites and were under the control of an English-speaking boss who could act as an intermediary. Lodged in boarding houses, the Japanese provided a ready pool of workers. By 1901, it was reported that Japanese made up 25 percent of the workforce in lumber and shingle mills.[6] While many of these immigrants may have come from farming communities, there was little chance to buy or lease a farm, so the rough and dangerous jobs in coal mines or lumber camps were the only options available.

So it was for Tow Inouye. By about 1906, he moved away from the coast and into the "upper country" of the valleys in the Rocky Mountains to work in lumbering. Timber from adjacent forests was being floated down the

North Thompson River to Shuswap Lake for processing by several sawmills, including the Adams River Lumber Company, near the town of Chase. Inouye caught on at the mill and lived in the nearby city of Kamloops. Set at the confluence of the two branches of the Thompson River, Kamloops was a jewel of a city, the self-described inland capital of the Rockies. Not long after Inouye arrived in the area, the local newspaper, the *Kamloops Standard*, bragged of the municipality's modernity. It had electric lights, a waterworks system, a modern hospital, and was "the administrative centre for a large and populous district," the main selling point being that the "district surrounding the city is rich in all the resources which make for the up-building of a prosperous community."[7]

Much of the labour that generated this prosperity was from lumbering, which was supplied by a small army of Asian workers, most of them Chinese. Kamloops had had a Chinese community since 1887, which totalled four hundred residents by 1890. It was estimated that by the 1890s, one-third of the city's population was Chinese. While many Chinese men began as railway workers, many of them became permanent residents and moved on to work at the lumber mills. Newly arrived Japanese workers were hired initially at cheaper rates than the Chinese and supplanted them at many sites. The two ethnic groups retained their distinct identities, and there was little fraternizing: "The Japanese had always considered themselves as separate from the Chinese as they were from other groups. Certainly at no time in the early years of settlement did they attempt to pool their resources in an effort to combat the grievances they had in common."[8]

While Asians made up an indispensable part of this burgeoning economy, they were seldom seen. Living apart in small groups, the Japanese spoke their own language and lived much as they had in the old country. They were not able, or for that matter allowed, to assimilate into the wider Canadian community. Hostility toward them was barely concealed. In October 1908, when Inouye was new to the district, the *Standard* printed a warning to the citizens that an influx of Japanese could be expected and that the Laurier government was indifferent to "the desirability of excluding Japanese immigration."[9] The local newspaper rarely commented on Asians except when the police would raid an "opium joint."[10] The murder trial of a railway worker, only identified as Takahashi, was one of the few acknowledgements that some Japanese even lived in the district. When he was hanged in 1912, a reporter wrote that Takahashi "received his doom with the customary stolid expression so peculiar of his race."[11]

Tow Inouye had been doing well at the Adams River Lumber Company mill, and by 1907, he was able to induce Mikuma Asada to leave Japan and join him in the British Columbia Interior. They were married on July 19 of that year. Born in 1882, in Kanazawa, Ishikawa Prefecture, Mikuma belonged to a samurai family.[12] Most likely an arranged marriage, the union was probably formalized by proxy in Japan until Mikuma's arrival in Kamloops. The couple's first child, a daughter, Esther, was born in 1909. She was followed in regular succession by three more girls, Susan (b. 1911), Martha (b. 1913), and Ruth (b. 1915). A son, Kanao — unlike his sisters, given a distinctively Japanese name — was born on May 24, 1916. There is some speculation that the first two characters in his name were taken from the *kanji* version of "Canada"; however, the correct *kanji* version of his name was taken from his father's home prefecture of Kanagawa. It is possible that his parents were honouring both places in their son's name.[13]

The outbreak of the First World War, in August 1914, stirred Japanese Canadians to action, and many young men sought to enlist. In Vancouver, the Canadian Japanese Association formed an impromptu volunteer corps of 202 men and, under the supervision of white officers, began to drill and train. Armed Japanese marching through the streets was an unsettling sight to some, as was the prospect that after the war these men would expect to be treated as full citizens. The "Japanese Volunteer Corps" was disbanded after three months. The reason given at the time was that there were too few volunteers to make up a full battalion.[14] After two years of carnage, the willingness of the CEF to accept volunteers, any volunteers, had undergone a massive transformation. On January 3, 1916, the minister of militia, Sam Hughes, announced the raising of "special regiments," and the *Vancouver Sun* reported that a full company of over 250 Japanese could be raised immediately.[15] Nevertheless, in May 1916, the Canadian government declined the offer; the stark fact remained that British Columbian authorities did not want armed Japanese in their presence.

According to writer Ken Adachi, the reasons for Japanese Canadian enthusiasm for enlisting varied. To some, it may have been a way to escape the tedium of the coal mine or lumber mill. Others may have thought of it as a way of advancing into full membership in Canadian society. Several recruits admitted that since Japan was also an Allied power, they enlisted "as a Japanese, not as a Canadian"[16] to do their duty to the emperor by fighting the common enemy. Each man had his own reasons and we do not know why Tow Inouye enlisted in the CEF on July 19, 1916. Unlike so many Japanese Canadians, Inouye did not have to travel to Alberta but enlisted in his own province. He was sworn into service at New Westminster, B.C., as a member of the 131st Westminster Battalion. He was volunteering to leave his four young daughters and newborn son to enter a war in which casualties were already enormous and likely to get heavier. He gave his trade as "merchant," perhaps a reference to his future aspirations. A note at the end of his enlistment paper simply says, "occupation lumberman — 10 years."[17] At age thirty-two, he was a robust man, five feet, two and a half inches tall, with a dark complexion. He signed the standard military will granting his estate to Mikuma in the event of his death.

With little more than three months of training, Inouye was shipped out of Halifax Harbour on November 1 en route to Europe. After two weeks in England, on November 28, 1916, he arrived in France and was taken on strength of the Forty-Seventh Battalion of the CEF, a front-line combat unit that would be his home for the next two years. Through 1917, he served with the battalion in some of the most horrific battles of that year, including Vimy Ridge and Passchendaele. The fall of 1918 would see the Forty-Seventh at the centre of some of the most decisive battles of the war. On September 27, 1918, the Canal du Nord was captured in a brilliant night-time assault. Inouye took part in this attack and was cited for the Military Medal for his bravery. The surviving account of his citation recounts that during the battle he encountered a wounded captain. Under intense enemy fire, he located a stretcher but was unable to carry the officer away by himself. Inouye charged the enemy position and overpowered three Germans. Using them to assist him, he evacuated the captain to safety.[18]

Barely a month later, on November 1, 1918, with the war almost over, Tow Inouye was badly wounded. The medical report indicated he was shot and sustained shrapnel wounds to the lower jaw.[19] Evacuated to England, he was sent to the Bath War Hospital, where he spent the next two months recovering. It was not until the end of 1918 that he was transferred to the Canadian Convalescent Hospital at Wokingham. However, he was young and resilient and by February 6, 1919, he was cleared for return to Canada. By the end of March, he was back in Vancouver and demobilized.[20] After his discharge, Inouye showed no interest in returning to Kamloops and the lumber mill. Instead, he collected his wife and children and resettled in Maple Ridge, a farming community east of Vancouver, down the Fraser River valley.[21] The Maple Ridge district was "formerly an uninhabited waste section of land, [which] became a thriving farming area — as Japanese farmers like to claim, 'a monument to their labour, diligence and perseverance.'"[22] His accumulated military pay and discharge bonus were likely the source of the capital he invested in a poultry farm. Socially and economically, it was a step upward. The work required was only a trifle less onerous than the lumberyard, but at least Inouye and his family were the beneficiaries. Inouye may also have been present for a memorial service on April 9, 1920. Three years to the day after the assault on Vimy Ridge, the Japanese Canadian Association dedicated the Japanese Canadian War Memorial in Vancouver's Stanley Park. The names of all Japanese who had served in the war, including "Inouye MM" as well as the fifty-four who had been killed, were listed on the cenotaph's twelve-foot polygon granite base.

War hero or not, the "not welcome" sign for Inouye and his family was prominently on display. Real citizenship remained very much an illusion. At a veteran's conference in Vernon, B.C., in 1920, a resolution called for all returned soldiers, including the 143 Japanese Canadians in British Columbia who survived the war, to have the franchise. In an open letter circulated to provincial legislators, Japanese veterans pointed out that as serving soldiers at the front, they were able to vote in the 1918 federal election. Why should that privilege be withdrawn now?[23] But it was, and the B.C. government would not extend the vote to any Japanese, including veterans. If anything, anti-Japanese sentiment became more strident in the immediate postwar period. Over five thousand Asians arrived in the province in 1919. This substantial, but temporary, influx again raised nativist alarms. In Merritt, a town near Kamloops, a returned sergeant-major, James Robinson, harangued a white audience with accusations that "enemy aliens, orienatale [*sic*] undesirable Greeks and others"[24] were taking their jobs, which was received with enthusiastic applause. In the House of Commons, a Colonel Peck warned that British Columbia "was getting more yellow each year, the Japanese were gaining control of the fishing industry."[25]

The Inouye family fortunes were on the rise in the early 1920s. Inouye Tokutaro, Tow's father, travelled to Canada in 1920 to visit his third son and his family. In the early 1900s, he worked for Wada Toyoharu, the president of Fujibo, and was assigned to assist in the refinancing and expansion of the Keio Electric Railway Company. The Fujibo company was compelled to assume the management of Keio, and Wada insisted that Inouye Tokutaro be made Keio's managing director. In succeeding years, the Keio electric trains became a vital part of Japan's new interurban transit system. As well, Inouye possessed the vision to expand Keio into bus services, leisure facilities, and amusement parks. By 1920, he was one of the most successful industrialists in the country. A photo taken during his 1920 Canada visit shows him standing next to his son, with his four granddaughters. Tokutaro appears

Inouye family, circa 1920. *Back row, left to right:* Tokutaro, Tow, Ruth, unknown, Mikuma; *front row, left to right:* Martha, Susan, Kanao, Esther.

stiff and courtly, as befitted a Japanese magnate, while Tow, in a western business suit, is more casual. Near the centre, and occupying the place of honour, four-year-old Kanao peers apprehensively at the camera.

Young Kanao began school at Port Haney Elementary School, in 1922. Shortly thereafter, the family moved to Vancouver, and he transferred to Seymour School. As for Tow Inouye, he achieved his dreams and became a successful merchant operating his own export-import business. Around 1922, he sold the poultry farm, moved to Vancouver, and started an enterprise exporting cedar poles to Japan. By June 1926, Tow was prosperous enough to take his entire family back to Japan for a visit. It must have been a memorable celebration, for the previous year Inouye Tokutaro was made the president and chairman of the board of Keio Electric Railways. Martha Inouye, thirteen years old, recalled walking Tokyo's streets, the only little girl in a Western dress. There was also an official aspect to the visit, for on August 26, Tow Inouye removed his name from his father's family roll and registered the establishment of a branch family in Tokyo, which was accepted by the head of Hongo-ku, Shibuya Tokusaburo. Significantly, Tow Inouye also registered proof of his marriage to Mikuma Asada. She had also previously registered Kanao's birth with the Japanese consul in Vancouver, in February 1918, which established Kanao in his father's new branch family and entitled him to a Japanese passport.[26] While these acts may have seemed mere formalities at the time, they would assume significant importance in later events.

A sudden tragedy struck the family when Tow Inouye fell ill, likely of appendicitis, and died on September 10, 1926, at Surugadai Hospital, in Tokyo. He was buried in the family's ancestral cemetery in Atsugi, in Kanagawa Prefecture. As per tradition, Kanao was thereafter registered as the *koshu*, or head of the family, at their Tokyo address. After the family's return to British Columbia, Kanao went to Templeton Technical High School from 1929 to 1932, and then to Vancouver Technical High School. Selection for these trade schools indicated that authorities were steering Kanao away from academics and toward a skilled labouring job. Van Tech, as it was known, was a mostly male, predominantly Anglo-Saxon school. However, it had a significant Japanese Canadian minority that figured prominently in all school activities from rugby to the camera club. For his part, Kanao Inouye did not stand out in any activities and finished in 1935, having completed only as far as grade 9.[27]

Despite his scant record of accomplishments, Mikuma had ambitions for her son. As her family came from samurai status, perhaps there might be better prospects for her only son back in the homeland. Inouye Tokutaro had been sending Kanao a separate stipend for his use, and it appeared that he had great hopes for his grandson and was prepared to foster his business career. Indeed, having a foot in both Japan and North America would have given Kanao a tremendous advantage and enabled him to rise in the growing commercial relations between East and West. In 1935, the year he finished with technical school, Kanao travelled to Japan on a Japanese passport and became his grandfather's ward.[28] By the 1930s, Japan was an industrialized and commercially sophisticated nation. It suffered less than most industrial countries during the Great Depression, and its gross domestic product continued to expand by 5 percent through the decade. One mark of this success, the Keio Electric Railway was only one of many private railways that linked neighbourhoods to the expanding urban metropolises.[29]

By the late 1930s, Japan also had a strongly xenophobic culture. There had been a rapid increase in military spending and a growing media frenzy proclaiming that Japan was surrounded by hostile countries. In February 1936, not long after Kanao Inouye arrived in the country, radical young army officers attempted a coup and assassinated several high-ranking members of the government.[30] In order to re-establish stability, senior military staff were granted greater authority, and the nation fell firmly into the grip of the generals and admirals. Inouye arrived in a Japan that was in "a toxic situation where most of its politicians, military and public had become infected with 'war fever.'"[31] Two years after his arrival, in 1937, Japan went to war with China and a virulent nationalist agitation seized the country. Western values were considered decadent and non-Japanese styles were dismissed.

Despite his wealthy and well-connected family, Kanao Inouye found it difficult to adjust to life in Japan and its xenophobic culture. His main language was English, and it was apparent from his accent that he was a

Nisei, a foreign-born Japanese. According to the first version of his early life, he entered Waseda Kokusai Gakuin, a prep school, and attended for a year and a half. Transferring to an agricultural school in 1938, he began to learn about silk raising and hot-house farming. As well, he began to study Japanese writing but found the characters difficult and was never able to master it.[32] Inouye would later describe how the Nisei young men would stick together:

> And they [native Japanese] always came and asked what we fellows were doing in Japan because we were not wanted there. You know English too much, you know too much about things. In one instance, there was a Nisei reporter working for an American paper. I was going around with him and suddenly we were put into a cell by gendarmes in Tokio [sic] and questioned. During the questioning I was given the water torture, and since then my health has not fully recovered.[33]

It was Inouye's harsh introduction to the insular atavism of the Japanese gendarmes, the Kempeitai. Retreating to Inouye Tokutaro's mansion to recuperate, he felt embarrassed to tell his grandfather that he was arrested and tortured by the police, and he explained that his illness was the result of a baseball injury. Whether he was innocent or not was irrelevant, since merely being arrested was a dishonour and could possibly implicate his grandfather. The ordeal was so harmful that eventually he went to a sanatorium. Even so, his health did not recover, and he was sent to a hospital to be treated for pleurisy.

During the 1930s, even though many Nisei were enthusiastic recruits to the Imperial forces, some Nisei were considered suspect and therefore were passed over for regular military service. However, after the attack on Pearl Harbor in December 1941, all were ordered to register for service. Kanao Inouye's proficiency in English meant that he might be of use in other ways than serving at the front lines. In May 1942, the War Office in Tokyo instructed him to report to Hong Kong to serve as a civilian interpreter.

When he reminded them that he was ill, the officer in charge responded that "it did not matter because it was not a strenuous job." Inouye would only be an interpreter, and he would not be required to take the soldier's oath to the emperor. Besides, the officer added wryly, "maybe a change in climate will do you good."[34]

2

SHAM SHUI PO

PERHAPS THE OFFICER'S PREDICTIONS WERE TRUE BECAUSE INOUYE was first assigned to the Japanese Army headquarters in Hong Kong. His duties there do not appear to have been demanding. However, in mid-November 1942, he was transferred to the prisoner of war camp at Sham Shui Po to act as an interpreter. This camp held many British and Indian prisoners, as well as almost seventeen hundred Canadian survivors from the defence of Hong Kong in December 1941. For the first time in six years, Inouye was about to be reunited with a large group of Canadians.

The tragedy of Canada's "C" Force in the battle for Hong Kong has been told many times. Military experts considered it unwise to even attempt to defend the Crown colony in the event of a war with Japan. British Army staff concluded in August 1940 that it was indefensible and that resources could better be used elsewhere. Nevertheless, in September 1941, Winston Churchill formally requested the Canadian government to supply a small reinforcement. Ottawa agreed, and 1,973 troops from the Royal Rifles of Canada and the Winnipeg Grenadiers made up the bulk of "C" Force. They arrived in Hong Kong — minus their transport vehicles, which were on a separate convoy — on November 16, 1941, less than three weeks before they went into battle.

The Japanese assault on December 8, 1941, was devastating and it soon overran the colony's undermanned outer defences in the New Territories. Hastily taking up new positions on Hong Kong Island, the Canadians fought as best they could but the defence devolved into uncoordinated attempts to halt a superior and coordinated force. At the desperate battle of Wong Nei Chong Gap, the Canadian commander, Brig. J.K. Lawson, died leading a final, futile assault. In one of the rare displays of chivalry during the campaign, Japanese soldiers reverently buried his body.[1] However, the rape of women and bayoneting of wounded prisoners was far more common. One soldier from the Royal Rifles recalled seeing groups of six to ten men tied up and bayoneted to death. At the Salesian Mission, a medical compound that surrendered without any fighting, the male medical staff were herded outside and systematically butchered. One Canadian officer who was spared for interrogation was cautioned that this was only a temporary reprieve since there was a standing order to kill all captives. At St. Stephen's College, which was being used as a hospital, the advancing Japanese seized

Infantrymen of "C" Company, Royal Rifles of Canada, Boarding H.M.C.S. Prince Robert *En Route to Hong Kong.* Vancouver, British Columbia, October 26, 1941.

and killed the facility's two doctors. They then bayoneted the wounded on their cots. Nurses were gang-raped and murdered next to the bodies of their patients. Afterward, over one hundred bodies were cremated. A few days after Hong Kong surrendered on Christmas Day, 1941, the senior Canadian medical officer, Dr. John Crawford, and several other doctors were allowed to search for wounded survivors. Instead, they found "masses of dead who had been butchered — hands tied and bayoneted and so on — very rough."[2]

Most of the Canadians who survived were held at North Point camp on Hong Kong Island. A former stable and more recently a dump, it reeked of garbage and manure. Red Cross parcels barely kept the men alive, and these ran out in September 1942. Diseases also took a toll, and dysentery and parasitic infections swept away scores of prisoners. Medical care was largely absent. An Australian doctor who escaped from the Allied camps reported that diseases were rampant, and men were required to do gruelling labour on two bowls of rice a day. To him, it was "studied barbarism."[3] By the war's end, 195 Canadians died in Hong Kong's camps.

In September 1942, the Canadian prisoners were consolidated at the Sham Shui Po camp at Kowloon, on the mainland. The men arriving from North Point camp brought diphtheria with them, a highly infectious disease that often results in muscular paralysis and death. Beginning in August 1942, the disease quickly became an epidemic and overwhelmed the facilities at the Bowen Road Hospital. At first, the Japanese denied that it was diphtheria and refused to supply any serum. By October, there were almost 250 cases among the Canadians, with a mortality rate of 24 percent. Orders were issued forbidding the playing of the "Last Post" when a man died since the frequency of the bugle call was demoralizing the survivors. Dr. Crawford was doing his best to treat the outbreak with the limited means available. Nevertheless, the Japanese felt that someone had to be responsible for the deaths. One morning, Dr. Saito Shunkichi, the camp's Japanese medical officer, called for a box to be placed on the parade square so that he could stand on it to berate and slap Crawford and the other Canadian medical orderlies.[4]

Word of the brutal treatment of Allied prisoners was first made public on March 10, 1942, by the British foreign secretary, Anthony Eden.

He reported to a hushed House of Commons that the government had reliable reports that after the fighting in Hong Kong, the prisoners were "bound hand and foot and then bayoneted to death" and "both Asiatic and European women were raped and murdered."[5] To the Japanese Canadian newspaper the *New Canadian*, the Eden report came as "a terrible shock to every person of Japanese descent in Canada.... There can be no mistaking the aroused temper of a large section of people along the Pacific Coast."[6] To their relief, the government made it clear that retaliation would not be tolerated since escalating rounds of violence could only further endanger Canadian prisoners in Japanese hands.

Even before Pearl Harbor, the Japanese Canadian community on the West Coast was experiencing increased hostility. Prior to the war, security agencies had only a vague understanding of any threat existing among the Japanese Canadian community. The hysteria created by the war did much to enable the mass expulsions of Japanese Canadians. As historian Ann Sunahara noted, "the attack on Pearl Harbor became the justification to fire many Japanese and seize their means of livelihood, giving those who hated Japanese Canadians an excuse to parade their hatred."[7] In British Columbia, those fishing boats owned by ethnic Japanese were seized. In February 1942, the federal cabinet ordered the twenty-two thousand Japanese Canadians residing within one hundred miles of the Pacific coast to be removed. Expelled from their homes, they were stripped of their property, confined to camps, and dispersed across the country.

Half a world away in Hong Kong, Canadian prisoners were enduring horrific conditions. Prisoners died of malnutrition and disease, and severe beatings by the guards were a regular feature of camp life. An account of American prisoners showed how pervasive mistreatment was. It seemed that the beatings, for trivial or no reasons at all, never ended. Clever prisoners learned to go down on the first blow to try and limit the number of successors. If the Japanese guards were feeling lazy, they might order the prisoners to strike each other and then beat up the ones they felt were not putting enough effort into it. At Sham Shui Po, one Canadian officer, Frank Power — the son of a senior Canadian politician, C.G. "Chubby" Power — saw guards stop Chinese civilians who came too near the camp. Frequently, these civilians were summarily bayoneted and their bodies tossed into the sea. "Women and children were often in this category," he observed.[8] The extent and brutality of the violence inflicted by the Imperial Japanese Army on prisoners and civilians remains difficult to comprehend. A quarter of all prisoners in Japanese hands would die. Most of them would perish through malnutrition, overwork, or random brutality.

The violence inflicted on the prisoners reflected their guards' training and the culture of the Japanese military. Recruits in the Japanese army were relentlessly beaten. Even after they began their regular service, ordinary soldiers could expect their sergeants to strike them at any time: "Physical brutalization was especially conspicuous in the Imperial Army, where the most common disciplinary measure, sanctified by tradition, was face-slapping."[9] Of course, abuse could go well beyond that. Shortly after Hong Kong's surrender, a Canadian prisoner noticed a Japanese soldier idly looking at a book in English. Military police appeared and beat and kicked the man until he was covered in blood and had to be carried off by his comrades. The Canadian thought, "Well, bad enough to be a prisoner, but thank God we are not Japanese soldiers." Mizuki Shigeru, who became an author of manga graphic novels after the war, recalled that he was not in the army for two days before he was getting beaten on a daily basis. The reality was that "in the Japanese Army, discipline flowed downhill; senior officers slapped junior officers and so on down the line until the lowliest privates, with no subordinates to chastise, often vented their wrath on unfortunate prisoners of war."[10]

This was the environment that Kanao Inouye found himself transferred to in November 1942. It was a camp where diphtheria and dysentery were killing men every day. On the morning Inouye and another interpreter arrived, an officer named Suda explained that "it was a mistake we came there, because we were considered as parrots … that is, we had no will of our own and he said we would learn later on the way we would be treated."[11] This was soon made clear when the new men were regularly subject to beatings by the camp's noncommissioned officers. Inouye and his colleague tried to resign but were informed that it was too late. The interpreters were considered the lowest of the low, and brutality was to be passed down the line to those even more unfortunate.

One Canadian officer, Capt. John Norris of the Winnipeg Grenadiers, described the new interpreter as "fairly tall for a Japanese and of better appearance than most of them. He wore his hair cut longer than most Japanese and had I believe the honourary rank of corporal. He spoke English well."[12] In September 1942, when the Canadians were sent to Sham Shui Po, Pvt. William Allister — a twenty-three-year-old Montrealer from the Signals Corp who joined "C" Force on a lark with a pal — gave a vivid portrait of the new interpreter:

> We enjoyed in an odd way, the sight of a fellow Canadian,
> free and well fed. His boots were beautifully polished and
> he smelled of clean, strong soap-perfume to me. Slender
> and sleek, he fascinated me and drew me with the hypnotic
> power of a handsome, magical boa constrictor. His face
> was soft, smooth, his features delicate. I could see him as a
> boy, adored and nurtured by doting parents, their graceful
> flower, a fine student.[13]

Allister's account of subsequent events, written several decades later and far from an historical record, gives some idea of how the prisoners looked upon the recent arrival. In Allister's colourful estimation, Inouye was "a monster driven mad somehow, somewhere. Mad with all things white and Canadian. His craving for vengeance was awesome."[14] He related a speech that Inouye allegedly gave to some troops on how the flag of the Japanese Empire would soon be waving over Ottawa: "All Canadians will be slaves as you are now! Your mothers will be killed. Your wives and sisters will be raped by our soldiers and anyone resisting will be shot!"[15] According to Allister, Inouye would beat Canadian prisoners on the least provocation. Inouye explained to Allister what animated his hatred. When Inouye was ten, all the children in his neighbourhood were invited to a birthday party, "but not the little yellow bastard — he isn't good enough. Beat the shit outta the little rat, that's all he was good for, a fuckin' punchin' bag!"[16] As a matter of course, the prisoners gave nicknames to their guards. Some, such as the "Fat Pig" for the camp commandant, Col. Tokunaga Isao, were as insulting as they could get. In Inouye's case, the prisoners had early on learned that he came from British Columbia's Interior, so he became "the Kamloops Kid."

A vivid account of Inouye's attitude and drive was later given by one of his fellow interpreters. Watanabe Kiyoshi, or "Uncle John" to prisoners of war (POWs), was a Lutheran minister in his fifties who was drafted into translating at Sham Shui Po. Before the war, he had spent a few years in the United States. While Watanabe was patriotic and hoped his country would win the war, the malnourished, brutalized state of the hundreds of near-naked, haggard prisoners on the parade square appalled him. When he expressed these thoughts to a fellow interpreter, Kanao Inouye, he received an unexpected response: "My dear Watanabe, your pity is misplaced…. Pity them! It serves the pigs right…. I hate them."[17] Watanabe was taken aback, and hoped the conversation was over, but Inouye continued to vent his feelings: "I too have lived among them, in Canada and they despised me. I knew it. I could feel it. They humiliated me. I was just another dirty little Jap to them. But two can play that game, and now they are the pigs and I am the master."[18] It was beyond Watanabe's comprehension that any man could feel such profound loathing. A short time later, Inouye forced him to watch while he administered a brutal beating to a British prisoner.

Cpl. Ken Gaudin of the Royal Rifles recalled Inouye's words when he was first assigned to their group: "When I was back in Canada and going to schools, they called me 'slant eyes' and 'yellow' and all the names you could think of. I've got you SOBs now where I want you. You are going to pay for it."[19] True to Inouye's word, he made the Canadians pay, and Gaudin further reported on how Inouye tried to make life miserable for them. Gaudin gave no specifics, but commented generally, "He was a sadist, no question about it. He was so evil against the white man, against the Canadians, particularly."[20] Gaudin developed a deep animosity for Inouye, but he provided little information in the way of incidents or facts to back up his feelings. Neither did Sgt. Lance Ross of the Royal Rifles, who concluded that Inouye had actually killed "seven or eight" Canadians but gave no specifics of who or when. But there was no doubt that Inouye held an ongoing bitterness against Canadian POWs and gave out severe beatings whenever the mood came over him. As Ross noted, Inouye carried a wooden sword "and would always be whipping it out and taking the men and ramming them in the ribs with it. He was the cruelest — or one of the cruelest — Japanese I ever saw."[21]

At the height of the diphtheria epidemic, funds to buy drugs were provided by the Vatican. However, no drugs were forthcoming. A Catholic chaplain, Father Eric Green, made an official inquiry as to where the money had gone. Lt. Frank Power witnessed Chaplain Green being brutally beaten by Inouye for having pressed his inquiries. A British officer was also aware that "the beating he [Green] received left a permanent mark on this quite innocent man, who had no harm in him at all." Claude Corbett of the Winnipeg Grenadiers remembered a time when the prisoners were relaxing at a prohibited pastime, gambling. One day, Inouye leaped through a window and caught some prisoners, including "Red" Patterson, who had only one arm, playing cards. For punishment, Inouye forced him to lift seventy-pound building blocks and made him run the length of the camp all day long. Corbett stated, "Yeah, the Kamloops Kid was a sadist. He liked to pick on somebody that was already crippled." [22] He further alleged that Inouye caused three prisoners to be killed, but provided no details. In any case, Inouye picked up another nickname. He became known among the Canadians as "Slap Happy Joe."

Inouye's time in Sham Shui Po came to an end in September 1943 when he and two other translators were transferred to the Fourth Division in Singapore. When asked why, Inouye seemed reticent to discuss the reasons, but implied that they knew Colonel Tokunaga had dipped into the black market. When pressed on the issue, he mentioned the missing Red Cross parcels and that "he [Tokunaga] was scared that we might report him to higher officials."[23] Inouye candidly admitted that they had no assignments in Singapore and had nothing to do. After a month, he was transferred back to Japan, to the Fourth Division's headquarters at Osaka. On March 28, 1944, he was released from service due to his recurring chest troubles and got a job as an export-import clerk at the Iwai & Company operation in Kobe. This ended, at least for the moment, Kanao Inouye's brief and undistinguished contribution to Japan's war effort.

3

KEMPEITAI

BY MARCH 1944, JAPAN WAS LOSING THE WAR, BUT THE SITUATION was not yet desperate. The military still controlled a string of Pacific islands that kept the Americans far from the homeland. Nevertheless, the enemy was advancing inexorably closer, and the U.S. Navy's submarine force had depleted the Japanese merchant fleet to the extent that there were shortages on the home front. It was apparent that in the intensifying struggle, Japan would need every man — but apparently not Kanao Inouye, who was basking in the security of his clerical job in Kobe. Nevertheless, he desperately wanted to return to Hong Kong. At the subsequent legal proceedings, he would explain why — he was in love.

Ho Wai Ming was nine years his senior and highly educated. In her native city of Shanghai, she worked for an American lawyer, but was dismissed. She then married a British policeman, Sub-Inspector W.R. Parker, and became known as "Mrs. Parker." After their divorce, she evacuated to Hong Kong in 1937 and ran the Sakura café. At some point, she met Inouye and fell in love with him. When all the tea rooms were closed by Japanese edict, she became entirely dependent on his support. It was unusual to say the least for a young Japanese interpreter to embark on a relationship with an older Chinese woman. In the rigorously xenophobic atmosphere of Japanese society, the match was suspicious if not dangerously anti-social, for not only was Inouye's wife Chinese, she was the former wife of a British policeman. Moreover, Japanese law forbade Inouye to marry her until he could get a certificate issued in Japan, which he did after his release from service in 1944. The only problem now was how to reunite with her. Inouye got the Iwai firm to arrange for his transfer, and he arrived back in Hong Kong on May 1, 1944.[1]

There was one problem. Colonel Tokunaga remembered Inouye and the trouble he caused in 1943 and refused him permission to enter the territory. The reason for this enduring animosity was never made clear, but it seems to have its origins in Inouye's gossip that Tokunaga had pilfered the prisoners' Red Cross parcels. Inouye vaguely phrased it that the colonel "did not want things said about him."[2] Inouye tracked down a fellow interpreter still serving in Hong Kong, Matsuda Kenichiro, and through him sought to get back his old job in the prisoner of war camps. Tokunaga would not hear of this and threatened to deport him. Finally, Inouye talked to the Japanese gendarmerie. Major Shiozawa, head of the Tokko section of the counter-espionage detail, recalled that Inouye had no passport but did have a "letter of introduction from a very important military personage." In a territory where English was a common language, Inouye might prove useful, so he was hired as a police interpreter.[3]

The gendarmerie, as they were known in English, or the Kempeitai in Japanese, were a widely feared police force who secured imperial rule in conquered territories. In the weeks following the Japanese victory in December 1941, there was chaos and violence throughout the former colony of Hong Kong. The troops of the Twenty-Third Army were given permission to indulge in as much looting and rape as they desired, and hundreds of Chinese civilians were killed in what one observer considered "a taste of Nanking."[4] Not only were bystanders slaughtered at random, clay tiles were also cracked as women desperately tried to scale roofs to get away from lustful soldiers. While the victorious troops were relatively considerate to the British elite, Chinese citizens were left in abject terror. Once the horrors ceased, the Japanese army and navy entered a contest to see who would control this valuable port. As the first order of the occupation government was to restore stability, the army's police, the Kempeitai, prevailed. They were given the authority to intervene in all criminal matters in Hong Kong and quash any seditious activities.

As Japanese resources were stretched beyond their limits, the gendarmerie would often use regular Chinese police officers and Indian sympathizers to supplement their forces. The Indian community in Hong Kong had a significant anti-British element that was eager to assist the new rulers. For their part, the Japanese cultivated Indian locals and renegade prisoners of war and encouraged them to think that they were all part of a larger, anti-Western struggle. Despite hiring numerous Indians and local Chinese to assist them, the Hong Kong Kempeitai commander, Col. Noma Kennosuke, would keep a firm hand on where and how they would function. While they were in theory a branch of the army, the Kempeitai operated in practice as a separate entity responsible only to themselves.

Whether he knew it or not, by volunteering to serve in the Kempeitai, Inouye became a part of a service that operated without regard for international law. Torturing suspects to obtain information was regular procedure. After the war, one former member explained, "If you torture them, some will talk. Others won't. Torture was an unavoidable necessity."[5] Whether the torture eventually resulted in the individual's death was of little concern to the police. One of the principal tortures used by them was water torture, which was excruciatingly painful but left few visible marks. Dr. James Anderson, a military doctor, described the process. The victim would be placed in a recumbent position with a cloth or towel drawn over the face. Water would be poured into the mouth, and the only relief came from swallowing. After a short time, the stomach became distended with water. As the body struggled to avoid this simulated drowning, water would be forced back into the head, causing congestion to the blood vessels to the brain, and "the feeling would be one of suffocation with intense feeling of bursting pain in the head."[6] Water torture, as well as being hung up from a beam by the hands and being buffeted back and forward — the so-called airplane technique — were the preferred Kempeitai methods.

When all else failed, the suspect could simply be beaten, whipped, or burned with a cigarette or hot object. These last methods invariably disfigured the body, but there was a good chance that the subject would not survive anyway. Frequently, the object of the interrogation was not so much to acquire information but to force a confession that would confirm the police were obtaining results. Furthermore, "as the Kempeitai began to lose confidence in their powers to maintain security in the Occupied Territories, their cruelties increased in direct proportion."[7] Inouye was paired with a Sergeant Moriyama, and the two of them worked under Shiozawa's direction to ferret out spies operating in the city. The interrogations conducted by this pair would form the basis for almost all of the later charges against Inouye.

As subsequent criminal proceedings would show, Inouye took to his new duties with gusto and frequently seemed to take charge of interrogations. Far from being a mere interpreter, he relished the chance to take a leading role in questioning subjects and he would never shrink from using torture. But he was not popular in the force. One of the senior men, Sgt. Maj. Hayashi Sadataro, thought that Inouye "could hardly write Japanese. He was a bad interpreter."[8] Inouye was never assigned to night duty since his written Japanese was so poor he could not prepare daily reports. Hayashi had other grievances against him: "He kept a girl, and I had a quarrel with him because he stole some money and articles."[9] In February 1945, the Hong Kong branch of the Kempeitai was reorganized and Inouye was not hired back as an interpreter. His former boss, Major Shiozawa, did not recall the exact reason but heard that Inouye "wished to resign due to inadequate wages."[10]

With the war entering its most critical stage in the spring of 1945, Inouye returned to civilian life. As transport back to Japan was now impossible, he remained in Hong Kong and got a job as a clerk at Kuwada & Company. Perhaps it was not a bad result, for his wife was pregnant and he hoped to go unnoticed in the general flood of events. Inouye was one of the eighteen thousand Japanese and their allies who remained when Japan surrendered and Hong Kong was transferred from the Japanese back to the British Empire. On August 30, 1945, Rear Admiral C.H.J. Harcourt commanded a task force that sailed into Victoria Harbour and began the task of disarming

Lieutenant-Commander Fred Day of H.M.C.S. Prince Robert *Meeting with Liberated Canadian Prisoners-of-War at Shamshuipo Camp, Kowloon, Hong Kong, September 1945.*

and imprisoning the Japanese garrison. At the same time, gaunt Allied prisoners and internees were being freed. Within days of Harcourt's arrival, Hong Kong citizens began to satisfy their thirst for revenge. One Kempeitai executioner was found trying to leave the colony. He was bound up and thrown into the harbour to drown. Other Japanese soldiers were hauled off a bus and beaten to death.

By September 8, 1945, it was reported that 369 Canadian POWs were liberated from Sham Shui Po. Still, diehard Japanese snipers were lurking in the hills above Kowloon, and "corpses [could] be seen floating by" in the harbour.[11] A Canadian cruiser, HMCS *Ontario*, joined the Hong Kong detachment in mid-September. It was a time of jubilation, and on October 9, a victory parade through Hong Kong's streets featured acrobats, stilt walkers, and a contingent of sailors from the *Ontario*. To a Western reporter, matters might have seemed in hand, but most Hong Kong citizens were on the brink of starvation. The liberators did not bring supplies for the devastated population and discontent among the masses of unemployed was rising. A month after the surrender, an editorial in the *China Mail* titled "Bedlam" noted that the colony was far from recovered: "Dislocation is complete to the degree almost of chaos. Price levels are so high that sanity shudders."[12] Pirates in armoured sampans raided merchants on the islands to Hong Kong's west.

Yet order was slowly being restored. By mid-October, a welcome sign of normalcy was news that "Old George" Bing's popular tropical fish store, the "Kowloon Aquarium," had reopened. Another mark of the new regime was its stiff determination to run down any Japanese collaborators or suspected war criminals. The Special Branch of the police ran an ad in the *China Mail* asking for any residents to come forward with information on those who assisted the Japanese, even though most of the notable suspects had escaped to Macao or Canton. At the end of October 1945, Miss Rosaleen Wong, a popular society figure who had welcomed the Japanese military elite, was arrested and jailed. A suspected war criminal, Lt. Col. Kogi Kazuo, was captured and returned to the Queen's Pier where "bootblacks and newsboys jeered him."[13] Two former guards at Sham Shui Po escaped but were caught by a commando patrol, which had "so far returned every Japanese who has made a bid for liberty."[14]

As historian Suzannah Linton observed, the pursuit of war criminals also advanced the British agenda "as a means of reasserting its authority and re-claiming prestige over its colonial territories, including Hong Kong."[15] South East Asia Command, the British military force that faced the Japanese for the past four years, now moved to reoccupy former colonial possessions and was aware that it had work to do. Having been swept out of Hong Kong in eighteen days in 1941, it was vital to reinstill a sense of British power. Some wags suggested that the returning forces thought only of themselves and disparagingly referred to the military command as "Save England's Asian Colonies." Even though the Special Branch did not catch all Kempeitai suspects, they ensured that identification parades would be held to show the public that British authorities captured at least some of those men who tortured their relatives and neighbours, and to demonstrate that "they meant to make sure that justice would, very literally, be seen to be done."[16] The return of British institutions and the punishment of war criminals had to be conducted in a thorough and orderly way so as to impress the inhabitants and rebuild their confidence in the Empire. Inouye's turn in this process would come in due course.

For their part, Canadian authorities seemed to have little interest in pursuing war criminals. An officer from the External Affairs Department explained in April 1943 that "the question of war crimes is not of great importance for Canada."[17] It took considerable persuasion to convince the government of Prime Minister Mackenzie King to investigate and prosecute those German soldiers who committed atrocities against Canadians in Europe. Even after this decision was made, one senior official noted that Canada had no major interests to be advanced, and that its concern would be restricted to "any war criminals shown to have committed an atrocity against a Canadian."[18] In June 1945, John Read, the legal advisor to External Affairs, noted that 107 Canadian prisoners were murdered in Normandy, but he still concluded that "personally I am not enthusiastic about the whole war crimes business."[19] One wonders just how many murders it would take to catch his interest. Yet, thanks to the Canadian occupation force in northwestern Germany, Canada was in a position to conduct its own inquiries, and in June 1945, the No. 1 Canadian War Crimes Unit was created under the command of Lt. Col. B.J.S. Macdonald.

Macdonald's men uncovered numerous instances in which troops from the 12th SS Panzer Division "Hitler Youth" executed Canadians after capture. During the battle for Normandy in June 1944, groups of Canadian prisoners were herded together and machine-gunned. One person emerged as a likely culprit — the 12th SS's commander, Kurt Meyer, was put on trial in December 1945, and charged with ordering and encouraging his troops to kill prisoners. An arrogant, unrepentant Nazi, Meyer's stern face was on the front pages of Canadian newspapers day after day. Convicted of being responsible for the killing of prisoners, he was sentenced to be shot. When his death sentence was commuted to life in prison, there was outrage in Canada that clemency was being shown to this "Nazi butcher." For weeks, the country's newspapers were filled with accounts of a military trial gone awry. It was an example of what a political minefield war crimes prosecutions could be, and how a government, especially one as cautious as that of Mackenzie King's, should proceed.[20]

Even though the Canadian contribution to the Pacific war was far smaller than that in Europe, it was impossible to ignore what happened to the members of "C" Force. Even before the surrender, word of numerous atrocities was beginning to circulate. James Riley, a private in the Royal Rifles, deserted before the surrender, slipped into civilian attire, and sailed back to Canada late in 1943. While fighting, he had witnessed Japanese soldiers enter a hotel intent on killing wounded men who were being treated there. They were halted by Nurse Elizabeth Mosey, who ordered the Japanese to leave. Others were not so lucky, and Riley was shocked to see piles of dead British soldiers who were shot with their hands tied after capture. While he did not witness it, he reported what he heard about the St. Stephen's hospital massacre.[21]

By early September 1945, surviving prisoners were starting to arrive back in Canada, and their stories horrified the nation. William Moles stopped in Union Station, Toronto, and tried to describe to reporters what they had endured: "They tried to freeze us to death, starve us to death, when they couldn't, they quit." He also described his guards: "The Japanese are just animals — they're not human."[22] Two Canadians in a Japanese labour camp guilty of stealing a bar of soap were tied to posts, left outside in the winter snow, and beaten every day until they died.[23] At the Niigata camp where 89 of the 250 Canadian POWs died, a guard promised them that "you are here to work and you shall work until you die."[24]

All prisoners returning from Asia were interrogated to find out what they experienced and who was responsible for their mistreatment. Over one thousand depositions were received and of these over two hundred made specific references to Kanao Inouye. These interrogations consistently referred to "Kamloops" as the one figure who delighted in attacking Canadians. Tom Forsyth of the Winnipeg Grenadiers even kept a diary in which he recorded one instance of Inouye catching men gambling after work and then forcing them to "carry loads of brick on the double for several hours."[25] Corporal Edwin Barlow swore that Inouye administered many slappings and beatings to Canadian prisoners. Rifleman Frank Jiggins witnessed a particularly brutal assault on two officers, Captain Norris and Major Atkinson. Jiggins described Inouye as "well built on the slender side but very muscular and athletic looking … he walked more like a white man rather than an oriental. He spoke excellent English with a Canadian accent."[26] And yet there were bits of information that indicated that perhaps Inouye was not at the heart of all the cruelties that marked the POW camps. Lt. Frank Power of the Royal Rifles also witnessed the beating of the two officers. In his view, Inouye did not act on his own initiative, for it was the camp commandant who ordered the punishment. Power also felt that it was another interpreter, Studa (Tsutada Itsuo), who was the actual force motivating the other guards. Nevertheless, public outrage would fall exclusively on Inouye.

4

ARREST

ON SUNDAY, SEPTEMBER 9, 1945, BARELY A WEEK AFTER THE BRITISH fleet landed at Hong Kong, Kanao Inouye was arrested. A Royal Canadian Navy public relations officer, Cdr. Peter MacRitchie, filed a story two days later describing how this Canadian-born Japanese, "the most sadistic of all camp officers,"[1] had been captured. He alleged that Inouye had disappeared a few weeks previously when Japan's surrender appeared imminent. Now that he was in custody, MacRitchie provided a florid description of the prisoner: "But to Canadians, Inouye was the 'daddy of 'em all.' Despite his fiendishness he amused them. They called him 'Slaphappy Joe' and he knew it. At dusk sometimes according to one Canadian officer, he would appear at the door of a hut and whisper 'where is Slaphappy?' 'If we fell for the ruse, he would take us outside and beat us,' the officer said."[2] MacRitchie's source of information seems questionable for his description of Inouye's past was fanciful. He suggested that Inouye was a spy and that he lived with his parents in Kamloops until the war. Inouye frequently boasted to the Canadians of his father's war service and that he was decorated in the First World War. This at least was true, even though MacRitchie noted that the Canadians did not believe it.

The *Vancouver Sun* reported survivors' accounts of Inouye's mistreatment, including an account from a Pvt. Harold Atkinson of Winnipeg: he would "beat them with anything he could lay his hands on, saying 'Revenge is sweet. I used to be called a yellow ____ when I went to school in British Columbia.'"[3] The Winnipeg *Free Press* carried the comments of Grenadier John Stephens that "Inou's [*sic*] unhappy school days in Kamloops BC cost the Canadian prisoners of war in the Hong Kong prison camp some of the unhappiest moments of their stay in Japanese hands."[4]

Revenge was on everyone's mind, and that Friday, September 14, in the House of Commons, E.D. Fulton, the member from Kamloops, asked Prime Minister King if Inouye, "one of the most brutal of camp guards would be tried by Canadian court martial."[5] The Prime Minister replied that it was too early to confirm anything of that kind.

Three months after his arrest, Inouye was interrogated by a British officer, Maj. A.M. Carstairs. He confirmed that Inouye's father travelled under a British passport and that "all his relatives in Canada have British nationality."[6] Inouye also disclosed that he had powerful relatives back in Japan, particularly his grandfather, Inouye Tokutaro. However, the only Japanese identity card issued to him was one from the POW camp. According to Carstairs, at no time had Kanao Inouye actually been issued a Japanese passport. Neither did Inouye mention if he had served in the Japanese army.[7]

A week after the initial news report, a Canadian diplomat in Manila, P.G.R. Campbell, sent a message to Ottawa to officially confirm Inouye's capture. He learned of this through a conversation with a released prisoner of the Hong Kong Volunteers, Sgt. Arthur Rance. Rance, whose mother was Japanese, spoke the language and served as a conduit between the Canadians and the guards. For future reference, Rance described Inouye in the following terms: "Weight 145 pounds, height 5'9", lank black hair, greasy appearance, thick lips, extremely bloodshot eyes, wears glasses sometimes; walks with pronounced stoop and quick mincing steps; given to gesturing abruptly with hands; hollow-chested; chain smoker and fingers very nicotine-stained."[8] It may have been an accurate portrait, but it was hardly flattering. It was clear that Rance was not an admirer. He recalled that Inouye "went out of his way to be offensive towards the Canadian prisoners" and that "he continually directed very foul and abusive language at them and used the slightest pretext to manhandle and slap them."[9] Little of this venom was directed at prisoners of other nationalities. Despite Inouye's public antipathy toward his homeland, the sergeant noted that Inouye "was always talking about Canada in terms of praise and it is the opinion of Sergeant Rance that he would one day attempt to return to Canada."[10] It was an unusual observation, for it indicated that Inouye was ambivalent about his Canadian origins, and perhaps he harboured some latent desires to reclaim his Canadian heritage and past life.

The Japanese Canadian newspaper, the *New Canadian*, carried the report of Inouye's arrest next to reports on how Canadian Nisei were volunteering for military service. Now that the restrictions were being lifted, at least 150 had volunteered. The first group of twenty-one were all former B.C. residents who were inducted at the Toronto depot near where they had been relocated. When they enlisted, there were reports at the same time that the government was planning the mass deportation to Japan of all Japanese, both citizens and noncitizens. British Columbia's attorney general, R.L. Maitland, demanded that all Japanese Canadians should be removed as he feared "fifth-column activities."[11] Ian Mackenzie, a member of the ruling Liberal government and a virulent racist who, ironically, spoke at the 1920 dedication of the Japanese soldiers' memorial, now argued that all Japanese Canadians were potential traitors and had to be removed from the Pacific coast. He proclaimed that there should be "no Japs from the Rockies to the Seas."[12] In June 1944, the BC Canadian Legion demanded that "Japanese and their children be shipped to Japan after the war and never be allowed to return here."[13]

The national hysteria for dispersing the Japanese had directly impacted the Inouye family. When the war broke out, Kanao's older sister Martha was living in the town of Port Alice, on the northern end of Vancouver Island. She had two children, and her husband, a Japanese immigrant, worked in the logging camps. In February 1942, they were given twenty-four hours to vacate. They hastily left most of their possessions with a neighbour and were sent to Hastings Park in Vancouver, on the site of the Pacific National Exhibition grounds. Once there, the family spent six months in makeshift quarters while the government debated what to do with them. Most of the Japanese were housed in a former livestock barn where rank odours and fleas were pervasive. At first, Martha's husband was separated from the family and sent to work at a road camp in Tashme. Martha, her children, and her mother, Mikuma, were transferred to the lower Slocan Valley in the middle of the Rocky Mountains, where they first lived in tents. Slocan had few accommodations, and the internees lived in miners' barracks and old hotels. Many worked at the farms of the nearby Popoff internment camp. After three or four months, they managed to move into a wood frame cabin. The Inouyes would spend three years in Slocan. Martha would give birth to two more children while in the camp.[14]

Aware of the anti-Japanese animus and hostility against them, and fearing that they had few prospects, by August 1945, almost seven thousand Japanese Canadians — including Kanao's four sisters — requested or were coerced into seeking repatriation to Japan.[15] In many cases, they had agreed to leave to avoid resettlement farther east among a hostile population. The community's newspaper, the *New Canadian*, stressed that those intending to return would find Japan very changed and foreign to them. It urged residents to stay and reject deportation as an "unworthy and needless admission of defeat."[16] Yet the *New Canadian*'s report on Inouye, the former B.C. resident and now the "most sadistic of all camp guards,"[17] seemed to provide at least some justification for the removals. Once Inouye was identified as a person of interest, the External Affairs Department traced the remainder of his family. RCMP officers suddenly descended on the Inouyes in late September 1945. In Slocan, Mikuma was undoubtedly taken aback by the sudden interest in her family and son. Inouye's mother was interviewed by a police officer, who reported that Mikuma had not seen her son since she had escorted him to Japan in 1935.

By the end of August 1945, Canadian authorities were aware that American and Australian war crimes investigation teams were being set up to deal with accusations against the Japanese. A conference of senior Allied generals was convened in London in October 1945 to consider a united reaction. It was decided that cadres of British and American prosecutors would be assigned to prosecute Japanese war crimes in various locations.

Once again, Canadian interest was minimal, and only a lowly major attended the conference. These prosecutors would apply the relatively new and pliable rules of Western international law to a defeated Asian enemy. While international conventions were largely under Western direction, Japan, as an emerging power, had come to play a role later in the nineteenth century. A party to the Hague Convention (IV) Respecting the Laws and Customs of War on Land and Its Annex: Regulations Concerning the Laws and Customs of War on Land, of 1907, Japan had bound itself to treat prisoners of war in a humane manner. It also ratified and confirmed the 1929 Geneva Convention for the Relief of the Wounded and Sick in Armies in the Field, which provided minimal standards of medical care for injured prisoners. These codes culminated in the 1929 Geneva Convention on Prisoners of War, which required countries to respect the lives of captured troops. While Japanese diplomats in Geneva signed the Convention, the document was not accepted back home. The Japanese Diet would not ratify the section concerning prisoners of war for several reasons. From the Japanese perspective, their soldiers would never become prisoners, so they did not see any reason to agree to a treaty whereby captured enemy soldiers should be treated with consideration.

After the outbreak of the Second World War, Allied diplomats inquired through neutral channels if the Japanese were prepared to abide by the Geneva Convention. They received a tepid response that Japan would abide by international standards. However, it was apparent even from the preliminary information coming in from Asia that Japanese forces had largely ignored the Geneva Convention. Chronic malnutrition, the withholding of medicine, and inhumane working conditions had caused the deaths of hundreds of POWs.

Public pressure to bring a measure of justice for atrocities committed against Canadian POWs was overwhelming, and Ottawa had to make some response. A War Crimes Investigation Section for Asia was created in October 1945. Investigations were initiated and preliminary lists of suspects were drawn up. But it would amount to nothing unless there was some process whereby those accused of victimizing Canadian POWs could be brought to justice. The problem was that since Canada had no occupying forces in Asia, it was at the mercy of the major Allied powers. Japan itself was under the control of the Americans, under the Supreme Commander for the Allied Powers, while the British sphere in China and Singapore lay under Allied Land Forces South East Asia (ALFSEA). Both Britain and the U.S. were willing to allow Canada to participate in war crimes trials so long as it accepted their authority.

In November 1945, two senior Canadian officers, Group Capt. C.M.A. Strathy and Lt. Col. R.D. Jennings, were sent to Washington to discuss on an informal basis how Canada might participate in the Asian war crimes trials. They were told that the Japanese trials would be under American auspices but that Canadian personnel would be welcome to participate as part of the American staff. While the most serious offences were committed in the Japanese camps and were therefore under U.S. jurisdiction, the report noted that some cases would be prosecuted in the British Zone. Cooperation with British authorities would also have to be agreed on but would likely not present a problem.[18] With these limitations in mind, the Canadian War Crimes Liaison Detachment–Far East was approved by the Canadian Cabinet in January 1946 and became operational early that year.[19]

Lt. Col. Oscar Orr was assigned to command the detachment. While he was respected as an administrator, Orr had seen his share of battle. At the age of twenty-two, he volunteered for service in the First World War and served at the front for almost a year, when he was badly wounded at Ypres. A piece of shrapnel hit him squarely between the eyes and travelled down his sinuses to his throat. Amazingly, he survived and later had the shard of German metal mounted in a stand with the inscription, "From Fritz to Oscar, July 16, 1916."[20] Disabled from further service and sent back to Canada, he finished a law degree and had a rewarding career as a lawyer in Vancouver. He again volunteered for military service in 1940, and for most of the war, acted for the judge advocate for the Pacific Command. But near the war's end, he was transferred to Ottawa where he gained background working for the war crimes detachment. Since October 1945, he served in the War Crimes Investigation Section gathering information from POWs returning from the Pacific, which led directly to being asked to head up the new unit that was destined for Asia. At age fifty-three, Orr was reluctant to stay on in any staff position, and with the end of the war in sight, he had hoped to return to Vancouver. When it was put to him that there was no one else sufficiently qualified, he reluctantly agreed to go.

In a revealing comment to the secretary of the War Crimes Advisory Committee in December 1945, Orr tried to explain why the Asian cases would be different from those under way in Europe. Orr had heard the disturbing suggestion that only those cases where prisoners had been killed or permanently disabled were to be pursued, and he felt that this was a profound mistake. Serious, even fatal results could follow from severe mistreatment. The Germans had not gone out of their way to humiliate or ridicule their captives, as "the Germans were dealing with another white race [emphasis in original]. The Japanese, on the other hand, in the vast majority of cases submitted our men to over three years of constant brutality and beating." The result of this brutality on men who were already far gone on malnutrition and disease was to cause their slow death. Those guards who had beaten and humiliated prisoners who later died should not be allowed to escape the consequences of their crimes solely because they had not directly killed anyone. Orr gave one prime example:

> The notorious Kanao Inouye, alias Kamloops Kid, Vancouver Kid, Kamloops, etc, has been widely publicized throughout the breadth and length of the US and Canada as a man with a hatred against the Canadians who took a special delight in beating them. He beat many — Maj Atkinson, Capt Norris and dozens of others. Many of the victims were given hospital treatment at the time BUT [emphasis in original] as far as I know there is not a single case where permanent disability has followed.[21]

Even at this early stage, Kanao Inouye distinguished himself as being a prime candidate responsible for the horrors of the POW camps. Orr had also put his finger on one of the main concerns — however unpleasant Inouye may have been, it was entirely possible that he did not kill or disable anyone.

It seemed unlikely that the death penalty would be applied to any accused war criminal who had not taken a life.

While Ottawa at last agreed to play a part in war crimes prosecutions in Asia, it was a small part. The detachment consisted of only four officers. In addition to Orr and his second in command, Maj. George Puddicombe, there were two junior military lawyers, John Boland and John Dickey. They would be assisted by two support staff and two noncommissioned officers (NCOs) who were former POWs. The latter not only assisted in organizing the cases but also provided first-hand evidence on the Japanese labour camps. One of them, Sgt. Maj. Harold Shepherd of the Royal Rifles, was a keen observer of the guards at the Omine camp and was even bayoneted by one of them during an argument. Due to Canada's lack of an occupation force, the detachment could only operate under American or British auspices. It was a modest effort that reflected Ottawa's determination to be seen to play a limited role in the international effort to try war criminals, as well as to assure the Canadian survivors of the POW camps that a measure of justice would be applied. It was a small enough force to avoid risk and cost, but enough to say that something was being done.

Lieutenant Colonel Orr and his tiny staff arrived in Tokyo on April 15, 1946. Two of the most infamous labour camps in Japan, Omine (known in Japan as Kawasaki Omine) and Niigata, would be the primary focus of Canada's efforts. Many Canadians were brutalized at both places and the two NCOs on Orr's staff could give first-hand testimony on the conditions at the labour camps. Ten days after the others settled into Japan, Orr, Puddicombe, and his chief clerk, Sgt. Maj. Arthur Hogg, flew on to Hong Kong. Before they left Canada, it was determined that Puddicombe would head up Canada's mission to Hong Kong. One reporter described Puddicombe as a "six-footer with graying hair and bristling moustache."[22] As with Lieutenant Colonel Orr, Puddicombe had also served in combat in the First World War. Volunteering at the age of eighteen, he survived several battles, including one in 1918 in which Tow Inouye was badly wounded. There is no indication that the two men ever met. After the war, Puddicombe received a B.A. from McGill in 1923 and a bachelor of civil law in 1926. His law practice in Montreal assured him an affluent and highly respected lifestyle. Nevertheless, at the outbreak of the war, he left his comfortable surroundings for a series of military staff jobs. Well beyond the age for combat service, he became the paymaster for the Victoria Rifles. It was his role as president of the courts martial for the Montreal and Petawawa districts that gave him experience with military law as well as its application in the courtroom. For this work, he was promoted to major in 1943.[23] A tall, commanding presence in the courtroom, Puddicombe was a fortunate choice for the prosecution staff.

The Canadians were welcomed by Lieutenant Colonel Minshull-Ford, the commander of the British Fourteenth War Crimes Investigation Unit, as well as by the Hong Kong commander, Maj. Gen. Francis Festing. As Puddicombe later recalled, the British investigators spent the war "behind the Japanese lines with the British Army Aid Group, the famous B.A.A.G." They were assisted by a cadre of police officers who served in Shanghai and

Major George Puddicombe (*standing*) with Sergeant Major Hogg (*to his right*), Hong Kong, circa 1946–47.

Tientsin, and "what they didn't know about the non-violent extraction of information from reluctant orientals wasn't worth bothering about."[24] On April 28, they sat down with British staff who had been investigating suspects for months. They were an invaluable source of information and freely opened their files to the Canadians. Orr only stayed for a few days and was off to Singapore, leaving Puddicombe and Hogg to head up the Hong Kong branch of the detachment.

The two men busied themselves reviewing reports and settling in. Within days, Puddicombe was tramping the hills of Hong Kong Island, trying to get a feel for the battle and the course of events. To immerse himself in the upcoming trials, he read over previous interrogations of suspects and victims. At Stanley Jail, the formidable hulk of a prison located on Stanley Peninsula, at the southeastern tip of Hong Kong Island, he interrogated several inmates, including the POW camp commander Col. Tokunaga Isao, as well as an interpreter, Niimori Genichiro, who was a suspect in several beatings. It was also Puddicombe's first encounter with the now infamous Kanao Inouye. As he later recalled, "For a Japanese he was of a fair size, broad shouldered and with rather pleasing features."[25] The inmates, all under the close observation of the green-bereted Hong Kong commandos, seemed reconciled with their lot. Puddicombe observed that "they were well-treated, even given opportunities to entertain themselves by way of sing-songs."[26] Ironically, the prisoners' favourite song was "There'll Always Be an England."

Senior British officers made it clear that the war crimes trials would start very soon and there was no time to lose. Assisting Puddicombe was Tse Dickuan, who was formerly a clerk for the Canadian Pacific Steamship Lines and employed as a clerk in the POW camps during the war. No longer just a name that appeared in so many of the affidavits of Canadian survivors, Puddicombe had finally come face to face with Kanao Inouye. The interpreter and the prosecutor were to see much of each other in the coming months. Although they were both Canadians, that seems to have been the only similarity between George Puddicombe and Kanao Inouye. The self-assured, successful white Canadian lawyer could not have been more in contrast to the nondescript Japanese captive. Yet, in the next several months, their lives would intertwine, and both would relive past events from very different perspectives. To a great extent, Inouye's fate would depend on Puddicombe's judgment.

5

POLITICAL FOOTBALL

ON MARCH 23, 1946, ALL 257 JAPANESE INMATES BEING HELD IN Stanley Prison stood erect several paces away from each other and waited while the residents of Hong Kong wandered through the yard. This mass identification parade was one way in which the British authorities hoped that persons would come forward and point out those who maltreated them during the occupation. One participant was Gonzalo Sang, who rushed to tell the British prison wardens that one of the inmates standing roughly at attention, Kanao Inouye, gave him the water torture. He further informed them that this same inmate tortured Enrique Lee, who had subsequently died from his treatment. The most voluble accuser to appear with information on Inouye was Rampal Ghilote, who swore that the prisoner on the parade square "gave me the water-torture, hung me up for 16 hours, burned me with lighted cigarettes, whipped me and made me stand up for three days without sleep."[1] Ghilote could also testify to other persons whom he saw tortured by Inouye. It was enough for Inouye to be selected as a prime candidate for the upcoming war crimes trials by British military courts.[2]

In the meantime, Inouye played a part in one of the initial trials of an alleged torturer. On April 2, 1946, George Wong was brought before the

Hong Kong Supreme Court to face a charge of treason. Chinese by origin, Wong had lived for several years in the United States and spoke colloquial English. Before the war, he ran a Hong Kong auto repair shop. After the Japanese conquest, he emerged as an avid supporter of the new regime. He once confessed to a colleague, "I hate the Americans. That is when I tore up my American papers.... This is a race war between the yellow race and the white race."[3] He wore the armband of the Koa Kikan, an organization that supported, and provided information for the Japanese military abroad. While he began his police career as a driver, Wong's support went so far as assisting the local branch of the Kempeitai in their torture of suspects, eventually "winding up as the Kempeitai's chief local tough."[4] Witness after witness testified to Wong's enthusiastic beatings of suspects under the approving eye of Japanese police.

On April 17, Inouye was called as a witness for the defence. He swore that Wong was primarily a driver or mechanic who occasionally assisted with translations but never abused anyone and did not have any official capacity with the Kempeitai. Nevertheless, it was apparent from a host of other witnesses that the two men worked together closely during the war in ferreting out and torturing Allied supporters. Inouye's attempt to assist his fellow-accused by saying that Wong was just a driver was a transparent lie as was much of his testimony. Under cross-examination by Crown attorney M.A. da Silva, Inouye denied any knowledge of the nickname "Slaphappy" given to him by the Canadian prisoners. He also denied beating the Catholic priest, Father E.J. Green, who had submitted a letter protesting the diversion of a papal donation intended for the POWs. The prosecutor confronted Inouye with Father Green's testimony that he assisted in the beating and told Green that "this was in return for the treatment [he] had received in Canada." [5] Inouye denied it.

Inouye did not even know Captain Norris, one of his supposed victims. Much of this cross-examination would later come back to haunt him:

> DA SILVA. You remember Mrs Power?
> INOUYE. Yes, Sir.
> DA SILVA. She was taken to 69 Kimberley Road. Is that correct?

INOUYE. Yes, Sir.

DA SILVA. There she was taken into a private bathroom and given the water torture. You remember that?

INOUYE. I don't think so, sir, I was not present.

DA SILVA. If she says that you were present and gave her the water torture, you say she is a liar?

INOUYE. Yes, sir.[6]

Prosecutor da Silva was relentless:

DA SILVA. Many say that your particular favourite was to blow at the end of your cigarette till it was red hot and then apply it to the person under interrogation?

INOUYE. I did not do that.[7]

Interestingly enough, Inouye described how the camp guards handled a situation in which they found twelve Dutch sailors with contraband radios. The Dutch testified that they were beaten for hours. Inouye suggested that the guards decided among themselves to keep the radio information secret since it would only attract the attention of the Kempeitai. Instead they administered a minimal punishment of five lashes to each Dutch POW. For his part, Inouye denied torturing Rampal Ghilote, whom he accused of being an informer, and insisted that "I was only an interpreter — a machine."[8] When asked why he was trying to turn the tables and accuse Ghilote of having been a police informant, Inouye replied, "Because we want justice, don't we? He [Ghilote] got innocent people in trouble during the occupation and now he wants to get innocent people in trouble again."[9] It was the beginning of a series of confrontations between the two men.

For the first time, the issue of loyalty to the Crown was raised. Wong was charged under the British Treason Act of 1351, a medieval statute that was designed to punish those subjects of the king who aided and assisted his enemies. What did this have to do with an obscure Chinese auto mechanic in 1946? Lo Hin Shing, Wong's defence lawyer, gave an extended lesson on the nature of citizenship. A Cambridge graduate, Lo was one of Hong

Kong's most respected lawyers. Three years after the Wong trial, he would become one of the colony's first Chinese magistrates. He pointed out that since Hong Kong did not become a British territory until Captain Elliott's Proclamation of 1841, statutes enacted before that could not be applied to Chinese residents and, therefore, Wong remained "an alien to the new sovereign." It was a subtle argument, but it failed to move the court, and Wong was convicted and sentenced to hang. Later that summer Wong and a fellow collaborator would be executed. For Inouye, it should have been a foreboding omen on the consequences of a treason accusation.

While George Wong was a Hong Kong resident tried by a local court, it was unusual for one country to set itself up as the judge and jury of accused persons from another country. When those accused were the losers in a recent conflict, the possibility for revenge instead of justice was all the more likely. But for the losing side, it was not unexpected. Certainly, since the Moscow Declaration on Atrocities in 1943, the Allies made it clear that they would insist that those enemy soldiers accused of atrocities would stand trial. And when Japan surrendered on August 15, 1945, it accepted the Potsdam Proclamation, which included a provision that those who had mistreated prisoners would be punished. Even if winning the war was a top priority, dealing with war criminals was not forgotten. The United Nations War Crime Commission had been set up as early as 1943 to gather information, but it remained up to the victorious countries to establish how they would deal with the accused. In the case of Hong Kong, the legal framework was a United Kingdom regulation, the Royal Warrant of 1945, which authorized the British military commander to convene the trials of persons who were accused of violations of the laws of war. In Hong Kong, that would inevitably include the actions taken by the Kempeitai against civilians.[10]

The framework was in place, and some of the accused, notably Kanao Inouye, were at hand. Bearing in mind the accusations against him of torturing Hong Kong citizens, British prosecutors had reason to see that he stand trial as proof of their determination to avenge the horrors committed against their citizens. If the British were intent on placing Inouye before a military court, Canadians also had a vested interest in him. In case after case, prison camp survivors identified Inouye as one of the most brutal guards who regularly treated them with humiliation and cruelty. Yet while the British authority in Hong Kong was eager to act, the conduct of Canada's government would be a monument to bureaucratic indecision.

On February 19, 1946, almost half a year after Inouye's arrest, the Canadian deputy minister responsible for the army, Basil Campbell, forwarded a report to the undersecretary of state for External Affairs outlining the information in the almost two hundred affidavits from POWs that mentioned Inouye. A number of sadistic beatings were recorded; however, there was doubt as to whether or not they caused any long-term injuries. Campbell also covered the question of Inouye's nationality: "Conduct of this sort by a British subject is treason: the same conduct by an alien is a minor war crime."[11] Already the issue of citizenship and who exactly had jurisdiction over him was presenting itself as a dilemma. As there were many witnesses in Canada who could testify against Inouye, Campbell suggested that he "can be removed to Canada or England without any difficulty."[12] It was a wildly overoptimistic opinion.

Two weeks later, the undersecretary, Norman Robertson, weighed in on the issue. Robertson was one of the most influential public servants in Ottawa and a key advisor to the prime minister. He observed that based on the known facts, it appeared Inouye was a Canadian citizen who committed treason. In light of this, "it would appear inadvisable to treat him merely as a minor war criminal."[13] Still, it was a legal matter and he referred the issue to the Justice Department to determine whether Inouye had broken Canada's Criminal Code. Deputy Minister of Justice F.P. Varcoe replied on March 9 that it would appear "the above party [Inouye] has been guilty of treason under the Criminal Code." But there were problems. There was a limitation provision, and proceedings could not be taken more than three years after the event. Canadian courts also had no jurisdiction to try a charge for acts committed outside the country. Varcoe added that Britain could try him under the Treason Act of 1351, an ancient statute that mandated death for British subjects who betrayed the Crown; however, it was difficult to prove and required rigorous evidence of disloyalty. He noted that an easier alternative might be charging and trying Inouye in Canada under the Treachery Act of 1940. This special war-time provision applied to alien saboteurs operating anywhere in the British Empire, and it was easier to prosecute and more widely applicable than treason, although the penalties were not as severe.[14]

After being kicked about from department to department, External Affairs was slowly arriving at a position. On March 22, 1946, E.R. Hopkins, the department's chief lawyer, wrote a memo to the deputy confirming that Inouye had in all respects conducted himself as an enemy soldier. While it appeared that the British had a claim on him, in Hopkins's view Inouye should be transported to Canada to face those prisoners he abused. "This man would appear to be primarily a Canadian problem, and it is thought that if he is to be dealt with at all he should be dealt with by us." If enough evidence existed to go forward under the Treachery Act — and there appeared to be ample — then the British imperial forces in Hong Kong should be requested to transfer him to Canadian custody for trial. The undersecretary noted at the bottom of the memo, "I agree."[15]

This moment of resolution soon faded when the army's deputy minister began to consider that perhaps the British also had a considerable interest in Inouye and might insist that he stand trial in Hong Kong. For that matter, he might well be on trial already. Other more delicate issues also came to the front. E.R. Hopkins seemed to be having second thoughts, and in a memo dated May 15, he cautioned his minister that a trial in Canada could impact the "internal political situation here, having special regard to the deportation, etc., of persons of Japanese race."[16] As Hopkins's letter warned, the political situation was delicate enough without adding a high-profile case for more controversy. Yet, on balance, Hopkins felt that while Inouye might only be dealt with as a "minor war criminal" in Hong Kong, he had greater significance to Canadians and should be charged under the Treachery Act in Canada. Hopkins captured much of the popular mood at the conclusion of his report: "Moreover, having regard to the cowardly and treacherous nature of his conduct and to the feelings of Canadians to whom he directed his attentions, it would seem desirable that an effort be made to have him brought to Canada to stand trial."[17]

The fate of this lowly interpreter was forwarded to the Canadian Cabinet on May 22, 1946, for a decision. Surprisingly, the proposal from several ministries to transfer Inouye back to Canada for trial was rejected. True to its cautious ways, the Cabinet was content to allow the case to play out before British military courts, for "established procedures should not be departed from for trials in the Far East."[18] It did not matter. The Hong Kong trials of minor war criminals were well underway, and Inouye was already scheduled to be one of the first to be tried. The Canadians could dither all they wanted, but British military authorities were determined to have their man. Inouye would stand accused of serious offences against Hong Kong residents, and he would have to answer for them in Hong Kong. Hong Kong's citizens had experienced first-hand the horrific actions of the Japanese military and police, and a reckoning was at hand.

6

GODOWN JUSTICE

JARDINE MATHESON'S EAST POINT GODOWN WAREHOUSE HAD BEEN used for the storage of commercial goods since the mid-nineteenth century. Originally built in 1843, it was still referred to as "Jardine Matheson's Opium Godown." However, the military trials would not be held in the old godown itself, but in a building near it recently erected by the Japanese. The purpose of the new structure was not apparent, but it was a spacious two-storey affair with large rooms at either end that could accommodate the courts. There was a verandah running between the rooms where, as Puddicombe observed, "Witnesses could wait and bored reporters smoke."[1] He thought it unlikely that the Japanese ever envisioned "its use to house tribunals sitting to consider the fate of some of their top ranking officers, and low ranking bullies of gendarmes."[2] The warehouse, while spacious, hardly seemed a fit place for a legal proceeding. Almost all the participants assembled on Wednesday morning, May 22, 1946, were in uniform, and it was apparent that what was about to take place was more of a military affair than a legal one.

Presiding over the court martial was Col. J.C. Stewart of the Judge Advocate General's Department in India. The other two members of the court were British officers, Maj. M.I. Ormsby and Capt. B.N. Kaul. Defending Inouye was Lt. John Reeves Haggan. Commissioned in May 1945 into the Royal Engineers, Haggan had not seen any fighting, and for that matter, he had not seen much action in court. He started his legal training, but it would be another four years before he became a barrister of the Middle Temple in London. Ironically, prosecuting officer Puddicombe, his assistant Sergeant Major Hogg, and the accused Inouye would be the only Canadians present for the hearing. Selecting Puddicombe as prosecutor had been one sop to the Canadians, a nod that this was a case of significance to them. He had been in the colony slightly more than three weeks when the case was called to order. It was a measure of the British desire to hold the courts martial of minor war criminals as quickly as possible and be done with it.

Colonel Stewart began by reading off the three charges (see Appendix). The first two dealt with an incident that had occurred at Sham Shui Po camp on December 21, 1942, when Inouye was alleged to have beaten Capt. J.A. Norris and kicked Maj. F.T. Atkinson. The brevity of the charges

British Army war crimes panel hears evidence, Hong Kong, circa 1946–47.

with regard to his conduct as a camp guard might have caught some by surprise. After all the publicity about the heinous "Kamloops Kid" and his violent crusade against the Canadian prisoners, only one incident was brought forward. This omission was not commented on but must have come as something of a surprise. The third charge was entirely different, but potentially more damaging. It focused on his conduct while as an interpreter for the Kempeitai, his torture of several civilians and responsibility for the deaths of four prisoners. To all charges, Inouye answered "not guilty" in firm, clear English.

Puddicombe then rose to give the opening address for the prosecution. The accused was not merely a civilian interpreter, but he was a staunch servant of the Japanese occupying forces who used his position to terrorize and even kill helpless prisoners who came under his control. The attacks on the Canadian officers Norris and Atkinson were done in full view of the Canadian prisoners of war then drawn up on parade. The element of humiliation, of white officers being thrashed by an Asian, added to the gravity of the offence. Yet, there would be no testimony given in regard to these attacks. Instead, the prosecution's entire case on these two charges would consist of a series of affidavits read into the record. The third charge, alleging that Inouye was concerned with the ill treatment of certain civilians, would be proven by witnesses. Puddicombe cautioned that this was a legal nicety, but in fact the accused took a major part in actions that cost four persons their lives. After his opening comments, Puddicombe proceeded to read the affidavits describing the assault on Norris and Atkinson into the court record.

On the morning of December 21, 1942, Canadian and British prisoners were assembled separately on the Sham Shui Po parade square. As counting the men had proven tedious and time wasting, the officers devised a system of chits whereby units of five men would report those on parade. According to Norris's affidavit, the Canadian battalion was two men short and a review of the companies revealed that the absentees were from his "D" Company. Two of the Winnipeg Grenadiers acting as medical orderlies during the diphtheria outbreak slept in and had to be summoned by a third soldier. The absentees came running onto the parade square but were not permitted to fall in with their comrades. This was a serious matter, for having soldiers missing on parade might indicate that an escape was attempted. Norris marched forward and reported this to the camp commandant, Lieutenant Sakaino. A slight, bespectacled figure who ran a tailor shop in Winnipeg before the war, John Norris was possibly the least imposing person on the parade square that morning. Standing by the commandant's side was the translator Inouye.

The Canadians' doctor, Capt. John Crawford, stood only a few feet away. Crawford was in charge of the Jubilee Building near the water side, where the diphtheria patients were being treated. Due to the lack of medical staff, many of the infantrymen volunteered to act as medical orderlies to try and save their comrades. When it became apparent from the roll call that two of the temporary medical orderlies were absent, Crawford felt that he was responsible. However, perhaps the camp commandant appreciated that Crawford was too valuable to be disciplined in the middle of an epidemic and instead sent for the company sergeant major. At this point, Captain Norris, the company commander of the absent men, stepped forward. He was aware that their sergeant major was ill and unable to endure any punishment, so he put himself forward as the one in charge. Sakaino began to ask questions, which were translated by Inouye. In short order, Inouye began asking his own questions. Instead of translating the commandant's questions, Crawford thought that "when Inouye took control of the situation any proper questioning ceased to be asked and he began to pour out a stream of invective and abuse." This led to Inouye slapping and then punching Norris. Pushing him onto the ground, Inouye began to kick him and called out, "Get up you world conqueror, and take it like a man."[3] Pulled up and knocked down two or three times, Norris was also struck repeatedly with a roll-call board. Crawford observed, "All this time Sakoina[4] [sic] was looking on smiling." When Norris was unable to get up, Sakaino spoke to Inouye, who was kicking Norris. Inouye paid no attention, turned away from Norris, and approached Captain Atkinson, the Canadian brigade major. Screaming out, "So your officers won't call their roll?"[5] Inouye kicked Atkinson on the knee. This time Sakaino called out in a loud voice for Inouye to desist. Norris later learned from an interpreter that he said "he would detail the punishment in that camp, that he was still Camp Commandant." It appeared to some that the commandant was becoming infuriated with the civilian interpreter beating an officer without any direction from his superior.

At the medical inspection room, Crawford dressed Norris's badly bruised face and was afraid that he might lose sight in one eye. Sakaino, with Inouye along to interpret, came to the aid tent, expressed his concern for the injured officers, and asked Crawford to do all he could to save Norris's eyesight. When he was finished, Inouye apologized to Norris, but Norris did not accept his apology. Norris did not lose his eyesight but sustained a break to his jaw cartilage, which, he said, "Still gives me some annoyance."[6]

Some doubt was cast on Inouye's responsibility by a further affidavit from Capt. Frank Power to the effect that "these beatings were authorized by the camp commandant, Lieutenant Sakoina [sic]."[7] Lt. Col. George Trist, who was also present, saw that the Japanese camp commandant did not interfere. Had the commandant ordered or at least condoned the assaults? Without the affidavit deponents available for questioning, it would be hard to tell. When all the affidavits were read, Haggan rose in protest. Why was the prosecution relying so heavily on affidavits, which the defence could not test by way of cross-examination? The admission of evidence by way of affidavits was unusual but was a consequence of the chaos caused by the war. It was difficult to locate witnesses or know if they were still alive, and even if they were found, they might be thousands of miles away. For those reasons, the procedural regulations annexed to the Royal Warrant provided that the court may take into consideration any oral statement or any document appearing on the face of it to be authentic. However, it was still unusual to make an entire case out of affidavits. While it has been suggested that the evidentiary rules largely followed English legal practice, the reality was that the admission of affidavits and hearsay statements from third parties severely inhibited the defence. Colonel Stewart waved off Haggan's objection and ruled that the court had complete discretion. It was a casual admission that this was no ordinary court.

Reading affidavits into the evidence made little emotional impact on the judges since they left only a passing impression of the incident itself and the nature of the violence involved. As the focus of the case shifted away from the prisoner of war camps to the conduct of the Japanese police on the people of Hong Kong, Puddicombe realized that he had to paint a dramatic scene to enable the court to appreciate the enormity of what had happened. He would do that through a series of witnesses who were all victims of the Kempeitai. Unfortunately, much of the drama would be lost due to the ponderous time taken for translations. As Puddicombe later recounted, even the simplest questions took up a great deal of time between the question and answer. A question such as "Where do you live?" might take five minutes between the original question and the eventual answer, which was made even more difficult because "it is literally impossible to say a simple 'Yes' or 'No' in Japanese." Puddicombe added a final comment that said much about his feelings toward the defendants: "Even if he speaks English the Nip is given to evasions."[8]

The first Chinese prosecution witness, Lam Sik, was a wireless operator, later described by Puddicombe as "that small telegraph boy"[9] who was arrested by two policemen and Inouye and taken to the Peninsula Hotel. Once there, he was immersed in a basin of water and almost drowned. He fainted, and when he regained consciousness, Inouye tied him up and placed a towel full of water over his face. When this failed to get results, Inouye attached two pieces of electric wires to his ears and announced, "This time you are the wireless operation."[10] Lam described how a Sergeant Moriyama was in charge and Inouye translated from English into Japanese for him. Subsequent witnesses would corroborate that Moriyama and Inouye largely worked in tandem during these interrogations. When the other police officers left, Inouye remained and accused Lam of using a transmitter to contact the Chinese Nationalist Army in Chungking. Later, at Stanley Prison, Inouye whipped him with a dog whip in an unsuccessful attempt to make him confess to hiding a transmitter. While Lam observed that Moriyama was in charge of searching for spies, it was Inouye who administered most of the physical abuse.[11]

Far more detailed evidence against Inouye came from Rampal Ghilote, an Indian civil servant working in Hong Kong. On June 16, 1944, Ghilote was arrested and taken to 69 Kimberley Road, and from there to the Supreme Court. Moriyama was convinced of Ghilote's part in espionage and recommended that he be shot as a British spy. The police commander, Colonel Noma, was hesitant to kill an Indian civilian at a time when the Japanese military was currying favour with anti-British elements in Hong Kong's Indian community. Ghilote was returned to 69 Kimberley Road, where he was introduced to Inouye. When asked if he could identify him, Ghilote vividly replied, "I know he was the chief torturer of my body and soul."[12]

He went on to describe how Inouye supervised the water torture and demanded information from him. After several ministrations of the near drowning, Ghilote broke down and said that he could take them to the house of a Mr. Power, where he used to go to get radio news. John Power was a retired official of the Chinese Maritime Customs who was interned along with his wife, Mary, in 1941. However, because he was an Irish national and therefore neutral, he was released. Ghilote directed the police to the Power residence in Kowloon; they ransacked the premises but found only a licensed radio. Power denied ever receiving any short-wave radio information. Frustrated, the police took Ghilote back to headquarters, where his interrogation and torture was renewed. Puddicombe asked:

> Can you say from your own knowledge what part the accused [Inouye] did in inflicting the torture?
> GHILOTE. He was the leading spirit in torturing people. Moriyama was only the figurehead. All interrogations and tortures were done by this man [Inouye] alone.
> PUDDICOMBE. I was speaking of the torture itself. I want you to tell the Court the part the accused had in the torture.
> GHILOTE. He poured the water and gave the kicking and slapping. There were no Chinese detectives.[13]

After eight that evening, Ghilote saw several prisoners being hung by their hands from a beam. Inouye assured him that would soon be his fate as well. Ghilote described what happened next: "At the beginning my feet were touching the ground but every hour afterward my hands were raised until my feet were above the ground. I asked for mercy but he [Inouye] said there was no mercy."[14] Finally, Ghilote said he would confess, but when he said that he could not admit to what they wanted, Moriyama and Inouye resumed beating him: "This man [Inouye] now and then burned my cheeks, tongue and all over my body with lighted cigarettes ... he burned my cheeks, tongue and my whole body. He twisted my fingers and stood on my feet with nailed boots."[15] According to Ghilote, far from being a mere interpreter, Inouye was the principal figure administering the tortures. This went on from June 21 until Ghilote was sent to Stanley Prison on July 1.

The prosecution's examination-in-chief rarely delved into the purpose of these torture sessions, but the Japanese secret police were on a mission. They were a tiny minority supervising a large Chinese population, some of whose sympathies still lay with the previous British administration or with Chinese nationalists outside the city. The police were aware that a paramilitary organization, the British Army Aid Group (BAAG), was carrying on a clandestine campaign to help POWs to escape and to forward intelligence on Japanese war plans to the Allies. Founded by the indefatigable Australian colonel Lindsay Ride, BAAG was the underground movement of most

George Puddicombe (*left*) with other war crimes staff before his discharge and return to Canada. Hong Kong, circa 1946–47.

concern to the Japanese. While many of the initial BAAG staff were British, many Chinese and Indians provided information within Hong Kong to the extent that "the British came to depend even more massively than they had done already on the services of the non-Europeans."[16] A cadre of skilled young men of Chinese or Eurasian background such as Francis Lee, Paul Tsui, and David Loie became the backbone of the resistance within Hong Kong. Moriyama and Inouye had been small cogs in the machine trying to ferret out BAAG members and quash any local resistance.

Moriyama and Inouye had not made themselves conspicuous. On the streets, they both wore civilian clothes, although Moriyama had carried one and sometimes two revolvers. Through their informants, they had come to strongly suspect that John Power was acting on behalf of the organization and operating a wireless service broadcasting military information, sending updates to the Allies. The various locals who regularly visited his home had been informants. Proving this was key, which was why Inouye had pressed Ghilote to sign a confession: "Before you sign the paper we want to know who is No.1, you or Mr. Power."[17] To Lam Sik, Inouye had bragged that he knew a lot about wireless sets and that he could find out who was in command. But it was apparent from the haphazard extent of the arrests that the Kempeitai had had little understanding of who was in the organization or who was in charge.

These arrests and tortures were connected to an espionage ring, which was apparent from a key piece of evidence filed by the prosecution but largely ignored by them at the trial. Barely a month after the Japanese surrender, on September 27, 1945, Mohamed Yousif Khan described his role in the underground resistance. A British officer, Major Clague, had contacted him, urging him to spread British propaganda and discourage other Indians from joining the pro-Japanese Indian National Army. At the end of 1942, Khan had been introduced to an Irishman, John Power, who was a clandestine British agent. Power had asked him to do everything he could to stir up British loyalties among Indian POWs whether it was at the movies or the mosque. On Power's instructions, Khan also gathered intelligence for him as regards shipments in the harbour and, damage sustained by Japanese warships in Hong Kong. By June 1944, Power had fallen under suspicion, and Khan — who was seen at his house — was likewise a suspect. Arrested along with his brother and a friend, Ahmed Khan, the three had ended up at Stanley Prison. Mohamed Khan recalled that Moriyama had taken little part in the torture but was content to let Inouye beat him and hang him from a beam. After they returned from their "tiffin," Inouye burned Khan with lighted paper and then administered the water torture. Despite the tortures, Khan had denied everything. Since nothing was proven, Khan, his brother, and the friend had been released in September 1944.[18]

Espionage was a capital offence to both Allied and Axis powers, and any spies apprehended behind enemy lines could expect to be executed. Six of the eight German saboteurs dropped in the United States in 1942 were sent to the electric chair after a perfunctory military hearing. As the United States Supreme Court concluded, "Without uniform or other emblem signifying their belligerent status, such enemies have become unlawful belligerents."[19] The provisions of the Geneva Convention were largely inapplicable to spies and their lives were forfeit if captured. Nevertheless, the Japanese had lost the war, and they were the ones now on trial. How they had treated unlawful belligerents or suspected spies was the question before this tribunal.

Under cross-examination, Haggan fleshed out Ghilote's story. He confirmed that earlier that year, in May 1944, he had been arrested by Moriyama and confronted with evidence that he helped smuggle a British agent to Waichow. Located north of Hong Kong, Waichow was at least periodically under Chinese Nationalist control. After receiving water torture, Ghilote had confessed that it was true. But instead of further punishing him, Moriyama had released him and suggested that Ghilote could help the police by finding the wireless transmitter operators who were in contact with BAAG. After they arrested John Power in June 1944 and found only an authorized radio in his possession, they had returned to tormenting Ghilote. They suspended him in handcuffs for sixteen and a half hours; nine months later, he was still unable to use his hands. Despite Moriyama's rank and the fact that he was an actual policeman, Ghilote still held Inouye primarily responsible. Ghilote felt that he had been set apart for severe treatment since it was important for the Kempeitai's prestige to say that they had captured the "No. 1." The Kempeitai had obtained a statement from Ghilote under duress admitting that he was a spy, and he had been sentenced to ten years imprisonment.[20]

Ghilote's answers became evasive when Haggan asked him why the Japanese took him to the Power residence. He denied knowing why he was there — he was not under restraints and simply stood about with the police investigators until Inouye turned on him and began to beat him. None of this seemed to make sense so Haggan pressed him: "They [Inouye and the police] must have had some reason and I am certain in my own mind you know the reason for doing this." Ghilote responded, "I have absolutely no idea of any reason."[21] It seemed apparent that Ghilote was withholding something regarding his relationship with the police. What he was withholding was not determined, but in any case, the police had lost patience with him.

As raw as Ghilote's evidence was, by far the most powerful evidence for the prosecution came from a Hong Kong matron, John Power's wife, Mary Violet Power. She recalled how on the afternoon of June 19, 1944, a party of several Japanese gendarmes, one or two Chinese policemen, as well as Rampal Ghilote, appeared at their house. She also noticed among them a Chinese civilian, George Wong, who was notorious for assisting the Japanese in rooting out suspects. The police searched their flat and arrested her husband. The following afternoon, they returned for Mary and took her to 69 Kimberley Road. Once there, they insisted that she confirm that her husband was the principal spy. When she refused, she was handed over for torture.

The picture of this fifty-four-year-old, pleasant, and amiable Chinese woman being subjected to a variety of tortures must have had a huge impact on the panel of officers. First, she was held down on the floor with a towel over her face. Water was poured over it until she vomited. She recalled that Inouye was holding her hand and checking her pulse. When the effects of the near drowning overwhelmed her, she was carried to another room and hung up. The interrogators slapped and kicked her for a quarter hour. When Inouye asked her if she was ready to speak, she said that she had nothing to say. She recounted what happened next:

[Inouye] took a cigarette and burned my hands and feet and cheeks I think about three times on the first day … I fainted and wet myself and they let me down…. They just let me lie on the floor for the night. They gave me a ball of rice which I could not eat …

Everytime I was questioned, Inouye was the interpreter. They said my husband was already dead. When they could get no more out of me, I was slapped and kicked and taken downstairs to hang for six hours.[22]

After her torture, she saw others who were also caught up in the sweep. Dr. V.N. Atienza was covered with sores, and he said he wanted to commit suicide. Mrs. Power admonished him to simply pray harder. She also heard Ghilote screaming. When asked how she recognized his voice, she replied that she knew him as the man who regularly visited their house to talk with her husband. After the trial, Puddicombe recalled Mary Power as "this little Chinese woman [who] might well deserve a niche in the Hall of Fame" for "she put aside her own agony to bring comfort and succor to her companions."[23] She was perhaps the single most effective witness against Kanao Inouye. Along with the Khans, Mary Power was released from jail on September 6, 1944. However, her husband remained in Stanley Prison.

As a postscript, Mary Power described an unusual incident that occurred sometime after her release. Before taking the ferry across Victoria Harbour, between Kowloon and Hong Kong Island, she was approached by Inouye. He paid her fare. She turned to him and asked why her husband was still in prison and under what charges. He admitted there were no charges and that they simply needed Mr. Power to identify two men. A short time later, Inouye came to her house and took a parcel of biscuits and food to give to her husband. She also gave him a pillow, but Inouye returned it a few days later with the explanation that the prison authorities would not permit any pillows. It seemed an oddly civil interaction between torturer and victim. Perhaps Inouye was attempting a more subtle way to extract information since the water treatment and burning had not accomplished anything. In any case, John Power died in prison on November 26, 1944.[24] Mary Power was never told the cause of his death.

Haggan conducted a successful cross-examination in which Mrs. Power candidly admitted that while Inouye was always present, he was not necessarily in charge. She called him the interpreter for the Japanese, but beyond interpreting, his role seemed to become blurred. She seemed unsure of many details beyond the presence of Moriyama (using the Chinese name of Sun San) and another moustachioed Japanese official. She could no longer recall who all these men were and who did what to her. When asked by Colonel Stewart who hung her up from a beam, she replied, "He was a Japanese soldier I think."[25]

Several other witnesses confirmed Mary Power's prolonged torture and Inouye's role in it. Ghilote saw Inouye apply lighted cigarettes to her as well as to other prisoners. After Ghilote was transferred to Stanley Prison, he was allowed limited contact with the others and exchanged stories about the tortures they endured. One day, he met John Power, who related to him how Moriyama and Inouye "would use him in a barbarous way."[26] Finally, after one session of sixteen hours of being suspended with his arms behind his back, being slapped, kicked, and burned, Power was taken before Colonel Noma where he was forced to demonstrate how to operate a wireless transmitter.[27] It may not have proven much, but the interrogators had a tenuous claim as to who was their Number 1.

A. Madar, the manager of a trading company, recalled Inouye at the police headquarters and that the prisoners called him "Yankee" due to his North American English. During his interrogation, Inouye slapped Madar and accused him of lying. At another point, Madar saw Inouye screaming questions at Mrs. Power and burning her with a cigarette. When Inouye turned and saw that Madar and others were watching him, Inouye called out, "You know what to expect."[28]

After his arrest, fifty-seven-year-old Dr. Atienza was similarly interrogated at length by Inouye. He noticed that rather than translating questions, Inouye seemed to be conducting his own investigation and that he took the initiative in asking questions. While he was abused by Inouye, Dr. Atienza felt that most of the torture was administered by the Japanese gendarmes.

Before the war, Hong Kong attracted many itinerant labourers from Central and South America. Among them was a young Nicaraguan,

Gonzalo Sang. While it was never explained, the Japanese suspected Sang — who spoke only Cantonese and Spanish, not English — of being part of the British espionage network. Arrested by Moriyama and George Wong, he was taken to headquarters. Sang remembered his second session of water torture, when Inouye demanded that he confess to hiding a transmitter. When he refused, Inouye redoubled the water application. Afterward, Moriyama ordered the Chinese guards and Inouye to stretch Sang's arms behind his back and hang him from a beam. Once there, with his feet off the ground, Inouye continued to beat Sang, causing his body to swing erratically around the room. It was his introduction to the special treatment labelled "flying the airplane." After a night of being suspended, Sang's hands were so numb that he could not grasp food for a week. Despite this treatment, he felt that the water torture was bearable: "I did not drink very much. As a matter of fact I did not feel very uncomfortable." A few days later, Puddicombe observed, "I imagine a man of his racial origin, a Nicaraguan, would be able to take it. It is something inbred in them."[29] Whether it was the inherent brutality of the Japanese or the patient endurance of Hispanics, the prosecutor was prone to accept and promote stereotypes.

One of the final witnesses, Lai Chak Po, a young clerk at the magistracy office, swore that Inouye administered the water torture and burned his brother, Ip Kam-Wing, who later died. However, in cross-examination, Lai admitted that in his observation, Inouye acted mostly as an interpreter.

Albert Guest, a forty-four-year-old government wireless operator, described how he was taken in during the June 1944 sweep. Born in Singapore in 1901, Albert Edward Peveril-Guest seemed the epitome of the British imperial civil servant. Since 1921, he operated wireless cable systems for the Hong Kong government. When war seemed imminent, he hoped to evacuate with his family to Australia, but they only got as far as the Philippines. Although Guest's grandmother was Australian, her Chinese ethnicity prevented the family from entering the country per the White Australia policy. The Guests returned to Hong Kong and were interned at the Ma Tau Wai camp. Albert Guest's knowledge of communications automatically placed him under suspicion. Upon his arrival at 69 Kimberley Road, he was stopped by Inouye, who asked him if he knew the other detainees. Guest denied it and Inouye slapped him so hard that he almost fell. Inouye then bound him up while Moriyama placed a towel over his mouth and poured water down his throat. When the towel became saturated, Guest could not breathe. As his stomach began to swell with water, Inouye jumped on it and forced water into his mouth and nose. The sensation was similar to drowning. Puddicombe later described the impact of Guest's testimony: "I don't think there can be anyone here in this Court who can forget the evidence that man gave. It was given in a manner that was quiet and he might have been a doctor demonstrating a clinical experiment."[30]

Significantly, Guest was also an acute observer, and he was able to confirm that it was Inouye who ordered Mrs. Power to be hung up and that he burned her in the face with a cigarette and beat her at length. While he lay in the interrogation room, Guest saw fellow prisoners including Dr. Atienza, Gonzalo Sang, and Rampal Ghilote lying on the floor in dirty, blood-encrusted clothes. As for his own treatment, the second time the water torture was administered, Guest began to bleed internally and it seemed that he might die. Inouye squatted next to him and said that if he would just admit he was a British spy, then it would all end and he would be on the next ship back to "Merrie England."[31]

It was now Friday morning, and in barely more than two days, Puddicombe produced an impressive array of witnesses who testified to Inouye's brutality. Moreover, several of them had also seen him beat or administer the water torture to others. The stories effectively backed each other up, and there seemed little that any defence counsel could do to refute them. Haggan asked for the rest of the day to discuss with his client and present a case the following Saturday morning. The court was adjourned until then.

7

ONLY OBEYING ORDERS

WE DO NOT KNOW WHAT HAGGAN AND INOUYE DISCUSSED THE REST of that Friday. Haggan was an intelligent young law student, and it must have been apparent to him that at least on the accusations of torture, the prosecution had a compelling case. A series of victims had given eyewitness accounts of Inouye's leading role in the sadistic treatment of defenceless persons. But there were several options open to the defence on how to approach this and deflect Inouye's culpability. One option might be to admit the evidence but stress that witnesses such as Madar or Lai Chak Po saw Inouye as merely an interpreter and Moriyama as the prime torturer. It was also an option to allege that Inouye was forced by his superiors to commit these acts. The rigid discipline of the Imperial Japanese Army made this a plausible defence. While the nature of these tactical discussions is unknown, a clue to the approach decided upon by Inouye emerged when the court martial reconvened on Saturday morning, May 28. It would be an approach that Inouye approved of and his lawyer Haggan all but disassociated himself from.

Haggan began by briefly reviewing Inouye's background and his problems as a Nisei in fitting into Japanese society. Inouye felt isolated and experienced the "very opposite from the treatment I received in Canada."[1] He explained that the Nisei were different because they had been exposed to Western ideas and had little patience for the "small things that the Japanese always talked about."[2] Skipping lightly over the years from 1936 to 1940, he went directly to 1940, when he was admitted to a sanatorium for six months to treat his lungs damaged by the Kempeitai water torture. Merely chatting with a fellow Nisei who was a Western reporter was sufficient to attract police attention. After establishing a background where Inouye was portrayed as a fellow victim, Haggan moved directly to the accusations that Inouye mistreated the two Canadian officers in December 1942.

While the affidavits presented by the prosecution were not entirely consistent, Inouye's prolonged beating of Norris and kicking of Atkinson seemed a matter of record. The two officers involved had vividly described Inouye's actions. On the face of it, it seemed most unlikely that camp commandant Sakaino authorized the violent outburst against the two Canadians. Nicknamed "George" by the Canadian prisoners, Sakaino was a shambling figure who frequently appeared on the parade square in a scruffy uniform with a sword dangling by his side. He was known to "hit the bottle" in the evenings and sometimes appeared with a humorous grin before the massed prisoners.[3] Yet, for his part, Norris considered Sakaino "very soldierly in appearance," though perhaps he was being generous. In any case, Sakaino was an officer and was not likely to appreciate a civilian interpreter assuming that he had a licence to strike a fellow officer.

At his war crimes trial, Inouye had a very different account of what happened that December morning. While the story of the two men oversleeping was consistent, according to Inouye it was Lieutenant Sakaino who was outraged by the missing men, and he held Captain Norris completely responsible. Sakaino decided that Norris had a choice: "Would he rather go to gaol for six months or get slapped, and then he ordered me [Inouye] to slap Capt. Norris."[4] A moment later, Inouye added that "Col. Tokunaga [Hong Kong's military commander] gave out orders that officers or any prisoners of war should be treated as ordinary Japanese soldiers."[5] This was questionable, as it was apparent that the Japanese recognized the military hierarchy and gave a limited degree of deference to Allied officers. According to Inouye,

Sakaino gave him a direct order to slap Norris. Sakaino even took part in the beatings, and it was he, not Inouye, who kicked Major Atkinson. Many Canadians witnessed this event close-up, and they all gave a completely different version from Inouye's. While Sakaino may have momentarily condoned the punishment, there was no indication that he ordered it. He had certainly not taken part in it and there was not a scrap of evidence that he attacked Atkinson. Indeed, it would have been unseemly for a commanding officer to attack a prisoner. It was the first in a string of improbable lies.

When Haggan asked Inouye what his choices were, Inouye replied, "I had to carry out the orders or get into trouble myself. If I had not done that [strike Norris] I would have gone to Stanley [Prison] for six months, that would mean death, you don't know how they [sic] would be treated there."[6] In cross-examination, Puddicombe got Inouye to admit that he said to a prostrate Norris, "Get up and take it like a man,"[7] a comment that Puddicombe repeated several times, not so much for what it added to the evidence, but for its effect on the court. The image of a Japanese civilian taunting a bleeding, prostrate Canadian officer in front of his own men was one he hoped to leave in their minds. However, the beating on December 21, 1942 was the only incident related to Inouye's service in the prisoner of war camp to be cited against him. It was hardly the Bataan Death March and compared to other atrocities committed by Japanese soldiers it bordered on the trivial. Neither Norris nor Atkinson sustained long-term injuries. Haggan turned Inouye's examination toward the far weightier accusations that he was a Kempeitai torturer.

Inouye's initial descriptions of his encounters with suspects were, predictably enough, to blame everything on Moriyama. It was the latter who carried out the beatings and water torture, while Inouye's role was just interpreting. He further alleged that many of the details were wrong; for example, the Japanese did not use whips since they left marks. When Haggan turned his questions toward the ordeal of Mrs. Power, Inouye became even more guarded in his answers. She was married to a European, a "third national," and Japan had enough regard for the role of Hong Kong as an international centre that such persons should not be mistreated since it would embarrass the Japanese. Even Inouye avoided contact with third nationals as it might arouse suspicion that he was passing out information. When Mrs. Power was put under the water treatment, Inouye denied mistreating her, and claimed that his role never went beyond taking her pulse and telling others that the torture was going too far.

At this point, Haggan interrupted Inouye's account and reminded him of something they must have discussed before the examination. Any lawyer would direct a witness to avoid a series of answers so lacking in credibility that they made all of his evidence worthless. Sometimes, the best policy is to admit the obvious and try to move on, but Inouye was determined to act otherwise. He denied that he had in any way mistreated Mrs. Power, and at no time had he hung her up or burned her with cigarettes: "I have a wife who is Chinese and is a woman. If I burned any woman with a cigarette, that would be worse than a dog."[8] When Haggan reminded him that denying the obvious would not assist him, Inouye still insisted that he did not abuse Mrs. Power. It was a position that strained believability. The damage was done, and it was unlikely that the tribunal would put any further value on Inouye's subsequent testimony.

Many other accusations had to be addressed, and Haggan quickly moved from Mrs. Power to a more equivocal witness, Rampal Ghilote. He went back to their initial encounter. It was Tuesday morning, June 6, 1944, and the new interpreter Kanao Inouye was in the company of a senior Kempeitai, Warrant Officer Shigematsu, on the Star Ferry to Kowloon Peninsula. The two were bound for the Peninsula Hotel, a fine example of former colonial grandeur and the site chosen for the surrender of Hong Kong on December 25, 1941, which now provided penthouse suites for senior Japanese officers. Once at the Peninsula, the two met a sergeant, and for the first time, Inouye was introduced to Moriyama, the man who would become his partner in police work. Joining the policemen were two Indian civilians, one of whom introduced himself as Ghilote. They got right down to business and Moriyama asked about the location of broadcasting transmitters being used by British spies. Ghilote said that he could provide information on bicycle-carried sets that could only transmit twenty or thirty miles, but he was aware of a much larger transmitter located in the New Territories to the north of Kowloon. All he needed was money to help ferret it out, so Moriyama pulled out a roll of ten-yen notes and gave it to him. Far from being one of the victims, Ghilote was a Kempeitai informer. If this fact was established, Ghilote certainly had a motive to get rid of Inouye, who knew too much about him.[9]

Nothing happened for almost two weeks. Then, on June 19, Inouye was summoned to accompany Ghilote and a contingent of police officers on a trip out to the New Territories to raid the Power residence. Moriyama found a Chinese man on the third floor with radio tubes. Other than that, the police did not discover a transmitter, and the only radio on the premises had a government-issued license. Nevertheless, John Power was arrested and taken to police headquarters. Accompanying him was Ghilote who would now have to answer for having failed to provide results. Strangely enough, the Japanese used two interpreters, Inouye and Nishi, to assist in Ghilote's interrogations. Inouye admitted that despite his years in Japan, he spoke the language hesitantly. Nishi was a native-born Japanese, and though his English was weak, he could better communicate with the Kempeitai officers.

Inouye recounted what he saw of Ghilote's torture. According to him, it was all handled by the police, and other than translating the questions and answers he had nothing to do with it. At no time did he burn Ghilote with a cigarette or bash him with a hobnail boot. For that matter, Inouye explained that he usually wore sandals, white slacks, and a Hawaiian shirt on duty, which matched his status as a civilian interpreter. As for Ghilote's claim that he carried a gun, Inouye denied that he was armed. Inouye refuted in any way mistreating Ghilote and claimed that all beatings he witnessed were administered by Moriyama. As for the others, he was neither present when they were given the water torture nor did he ever see them. At no time did he jump on Guest's stomach during the interrogation. As well, he insisted that Guest was the prisoner of another Kempeitai named "Kaki" and Inouye would not have served as an interpreter in another officer's case. Inouye also said that he never dealt with Gonzalo Sang since he could not speak Cantonese. On the all-important charge of killing John Power, Inouye denied even being present when he was interrogated. As for the prisoners who died, he rebuffed any accusations of mistreatment and maintained that in most cases he did not even know them.

While the prosecution portrayed Inouye as one of Hong Kong's principal torturers, he maintained that it was a misleading image: "Moriyama took charge and I was the interpreter. He did all the talking and I was just like a talking machine, interpreting the questions and answers."[10] If anything, he was one of the least threatening and most insignificant figures on the police administration. It was Moriyama who became outraged when a suspect refused to confess: "Moriyama got furious and took him out and gave him a beating or water torture. When I was interpreter at Headquarters I did not have any rank. When there was no interpreting to do I acted as a tea boy or sent around to buy cigarettes, run to the canteen or shine shoes. If I did not do that they would kick me around."[11]

•

It was now up to the prosecution to paint a picture of Inouye as far more than an innocent tea boy.

George Puddicombe was a cautious man. Before he started to cross-examine Inouye he approached one of the Japanese-speaking staff, Sergeant Roy Ito, and asked for a favour.

Ito grew up in the Heaps district of Vancouver. His parents were first-generation Issei and through them and a language school he developed the ability to speak Japanese. While his parents spoke longingly of their home country, it was all a puzzling abstraction to him. In the later phase of the war when the need for Japanese interpreters was pressing, Ito was assigned to the Canadian Intelligence Corps in Southeast Asia and promoted to the rank of sergeant. In early 1946, he was assigned as a monitor to the No. 5 War Crimes Court in Hong Kong. Ito — together with another Canadian soldier, Fred Nogami — met Inouye at Stanley Prison. Their initial reaction was one of intense dislike for the accused who had caused so much animosity against Japanese Canadians. Assigned to assist as a court monitor to the proceedings, Ito had a front-row seat. Prior to the cross-examination, Major Puddicombe approached him and advised him that he might be called to testify in order to refute any accusations that Japanese were being mistreated in Canada. The fact that a Japanese had attained the rank of sergeant was proof, to Puddicombe at least, that Japanese Canadians were being fairly treated. Obviously this was an issue that Puddicombe thought was worth addressing and if Inouye could claim mistreatment in Canada, it might be a factor minimizing his guilt. For his part, Ito thought that "the officer from Montreal had little knowledge of the terrible injustice done to Japanese Canadians before, during, and after the war"[12] and that his observations might not have been to the prosecutor's liking. In any event, the issue never arose.

Puddicombe began the cross-examination by asking Inouye about his life in Canada before the war. Inouye described it in idyllic terms — he was the teacher's pet in a series of schools in which he had received the benefit of a government-funded education. Throughout, he associated with numerous friends from the white community who accepted him.

> PUDDICOMBE: What about your relations with other kids in school? Did you play games with them?
> INOUYE: Yes, Rugby, Football, Indoor baseball, especially baseball.
> PUDDICOMBE. You had quite good friends among the kids?
> INOUYE: Yes.
> PUDDICOMBE. Were they all Japanese?
> INOUYE. No, most of them were Scots and Irishmen.[13]

This would be consistent with the Vancouver Technical Yearbook, which detailed the camaraderie between students of all races. Inouye was emphatic that he harboured no grudge against white Canadians. Yet, it was a version of events that contradicted the scores of affidavits that returned prisoners had filed. Puddicombe was well aware that in reality, Inouye held a deep and abiding hatred against white Canadians. Why Inouye chose to lie about his past and pretend that he was happy with his previous life in Canada is difficult to understand. Perhaps he felt that it deprived the prosecution of any motivation as to why he would want to beat Canadians. Whatever the reason, the lie suited Puddicombe's purposes as well, and he did not challenge it.

Inouye's backstory, as he now related it, was that he felt out of place in Japan. After his mother urged him to go there, he fell under the guardianship of his influential grandfather, Inouye Tokutaro. While he had many opportunities available to him, he could not adjust to Japanese society. In 1936, he enrolled in Waseda University and claimed to have graduated with a B.A. After his water torture by the police, he spent part of 1938–40 recuperating at his grandfather's mansion. He was too embarrassed to tell his grandfather that he had been arrested, so he made up a story that he was injured playing baseball. Sometime in 1940, Inouye moved out and spent six months being treated for pleurisy in a hospital. Thereafter, he attempted to learn silk raising at a gardening school but was unsuccessful. There was no mention of any military service. Although he was forced to register with the military in 1942, he was not conscripted due to his medical condition, and was sent to Hong Kong as a civilian interpreter. As his status remained that of a civilian, he was not required to take an oath to the emperor. On this occasion, the court did not have to endure the tedium of multiple translations since Inouye gave his testimony in clear, faultless English.

For most of the cross-examination, Puddicombe tested Inouye's story related to the accusations of torture. However, Puddicombe was largely unable to get Inouye to budge from the version he gave during his examination-in-chief. By repeating these claims, Inouye effectively implied that all of the prosecution's witnesses from Mrs. Power to Dr. Atienza to Gonzalo Sang were liars. When the cross-examination reached the evidence given by Rampal Ghilote, Inouye began to slip. He denied knowing why Ghilote was brought back to police headquarters. Puddicombe reminded him that he had earlier sworn he knew the reason why — it was because Ghilote gave them bad information on the location of the wireless transmitters. Puddicombe suggested that perhaps Ghilote was not a collaborator, as Inouye insisted, but was deceiving the Japanese:

PUDDICOMBE. So probably Ghilote, whom you brand as a collaborator, was making a sucker out of you and Moriyama?
INOUYE. Not out of me.

PUDDICOMBE. Oh, of course not. Just out of Moriyama.
He was kidding the pants off him?
INOUYE. I was only the interpreter. Just a machine.
Moriyama was not only the fool, he was the principal actor.
PUDDICOMBE. Poor old Moriyama. Ever hear of pass-
ing the buck, Inouye?
INOUYE. I did not pass the buck.[14]

As the day wore on, the contradictions began to pile up. On the previous hearing day, Inouye had sworn that Moriyama whipped Ghilote, but
now he insisted that whipping was not allowed by any of the police. When
Puddicombe turned to the testimony that Inouye gave at the George Wong
trial, many inconsistencies and outright lies emerged. At the Wong trial,
Inouye denied knowing Albert Guest, but now admitted to seeing him at
police headquarters. At the Wong trial, Inouye said that he could not identify Captain Norris, but now he confirmed that he dealt with him several
times and could easily recognize him. Perhaps most damning was his recent
account that he held Mrs. Power's hand while the water torture was administered. During the Wong trial, Inouye had sworn that he was not present at
all. For once, the court president, Colonel Stewart, felt obliged to intervene:
"Look here, Inouye, you must face up to this. At one time you said you were
not present. At another trial you said you were present. In which case were
you telling the truth?"[15] It was an impossible question to answer, for either
way he would have to admit to telling a lie under oath. He could only respond, "On this occasion, Sir."[16]

It was readily apparent that for Kanao Inouye, truth was a movable proposition. Inouye was fully revealed as an incorrigible liar and an unreliable
witness, and Puddicombe had what he needed.

Colonel Stewart posed a few additional questions, which did not elicit
any further information but revealed a great deal about the military judge's
mindset. Stewart first confirmed that Inouye was a Christian and had taken
his oath to tell the truth in conformity to those teachings. If so, then why
did he fail to stop the mistreatment he witnessed? Religion was apparently an important factor for Stewart, and he pressed Inouye on whether his

conduct was consistent with the principles of Christianity. Inouye responded that he could not order other people how to behave. He recalled an incident when an officer stripped a woman naked and beat her. Inouye admonished the officer but was ignored. Stewart persisted and asked him if he would rather die than apply water torture to a woman. Obviously, the abuse of Mrs. Power resonated with the colonel. Inouye replied that he would rather die, but that there was nothing he could do to stop it. Repeatedly, Stewart asked him what he had done to prevent these atrocities. Inouye replied that "I had no power to stop them … I was only an interpreter."[17] Stewart seemed unable or unwilling to grasp the reality of the iron discipline that bound the Japanese military and police. The officers and NCOs of the Kempeitai would never have accepted for a moment the right of a civilian interpreter to question their actions. Any hesitancy on the part of Inouye to obey their orders or, more incredibly, to prevent them from doing what they wished, would likely have resulted in brutal retaliation, imprisonment, and, quite possibly, summary execution.

Before he closed the defence, Haggan filed the list of witnesses he had hoped to call. The list included Lieutenant Sakaino, several Kempeitai staff including Sergeant Moriyama, and the other interpreter, Nishi, who would confirm Inouye's claim that he was just an interpreter. Given the fact that he was given the case with only a few days to prepare, Haggan submitted the list on May 17, five days before the trial began. He did not get a response.

Colonel Stewart considered the request and replied that military authorities confirmed that day that despite every effort to find them, none of these individuals were present or could be found. This perhaps was not surprising considering the chaos after a war, but it was apparent that given the limited time period before trial, no serious attempt was made to locate the witnesses. Colonel Stewart reminded Haggan that it was the policy of the Allied Land Forces South East Asia that proceedings not be delayed by waiting for witnesses. By way of consolation, Stewart said that he would presume that the absent witnesses would say those things Haggan claimed they would say and therefore the accused would not be prejudiced. How Stewart could possibly imagine what these witnesses would say defies explanation. The court was simply going to proceed without giving the defence any reasonable opportunity to locate those persons who might exonerate the accused. It was certainly a cavalier approach to any process designed to find the truth. Stewart's refusal to give any leeway on this point signalled a rush to judgment that denied Inouye any pretence of putting up a real defence. Whether he actually had a credible defence may be arguable but refusing any measures to allow defence witnesses to come forward effectively eliminated Inouye's chance to present an alternate set of facts.

There was little more that Puddicombe could add to his closing address. Returning to the treatment of Captain Norris, Puddicombe hammered the theme of humiliation. Before an entire parade of his fellow Canadians, Norris was beaten to the ground by an Asian civilian interpreter, and Inouye had the gall to order Norris to stand up and take it like a man. All of which was true, but in the full scheme of Japanese war crimes, it was hardly a major incident. Addressing Inouye's defence that he was compelled to obey Sakaino's order, Puddicombe cited the recent *Yamashita* precedent that superior orders did not excuse the committing of a war crime. Whether by design or not, Puddicombe was seriously mistaken in invoking this precedent. Gen. Yamashita Tomoyuki commanded the Japanese forces in the Philippines who committed gross atrocities against the civilian population. An American military court held him responsible as commander for his men's acts and he was hanged in February 1946. But Puddicombe misread the thrust of the case, which made senior officers responsible for the acts of their men. It had no relation to the question of junior staff having to obey legally questionable orders.

Admittedly, there were other weaknesses in the prosecution case that had to be addressed. Of the four persons whom Inouye was accused of having killed or contributed to their deaths, Puddicombe remarked that the accused was present when they were arrested or was seen during their torture. However, Inouye's involvement seemed tenuous at best. For example, the cause of death in the case of Enrique Lee was attributable to beriberi and not to mistreatment. Puddicombe also relied on the living witnesses who bore testimony describing Inouye's role as a torturer at Kimberley Road. Their accounts supported each other and showed that on many occasions, he used a burning cigarette, a whip, or the water torture to inflict incredible pain on his victims. The inconsistencies in Inouye's own testimony were glaring and frequent. Haggan's warning that being found out in a series of lies would render everything he said unbelievable now worked against him. Puddicombe worked himself up into a righteous conclusion: "He is a liar, a self-confessed liar. We have demonstrated that. He cannot be believed whatsoever."[18] Ending with a flourish, he asked the judges to imagine for themselves what he had done to his victims: "Think of the water torture ... think of these people swallowing water but without quick relief. It went on for minutes until they were full of it and became unconscious. I don't want to dramatise about it, but think of the horrors of the hanging torture. Hour by hour."[19]

This was not mere hyperbole. After reviewing the testimonies of Japanese interrogations and their aftermath, historian J.R. Pritchard concluded that far more individuals died from being beaten than from any other technique. Since the human frame is not designed to take the abuse heaped upon it by a session with the Kempeitai, "beating, at least at the hands of the Japanese during the Second World War, can be shown to be more murderous than other forms of interrogation or physical abuse."[20] Nevertheless, specifically attaching any acts committed by Inouye to an individual who may have subsequently died seemed all but impossible.

•

Lieutenant Haggan rose and took a decidedly deferential opening. A certain level of civility was expected between lawyers, especially from a junior to a senior, and he offered as a compliment that Major Puddicombe displayed the "superb coolness of manner and commonsense for which most of his nation are famous."[21] Interestingly, Haggan began his address by citing a venerable legal authority, Henry Wheaton's *Elements of International Law*. This 1916 text noted that international law applied to states but was not binding on individuals. It was a credit to Haggan that he managed to dig up this dated authority. But given the advances in international law since 1916, there was no serious question that individuals were also responsible for breaches of the laws of war. This certainly applied to the beatings given to Norris and

Atkinson on the parade square at Sham Shui Po camp in December 1942. Haggan argued that it was proven that the staff had to treat all prisoners the same — officers and men alike — and in beating Norris, Inouye was only obeying a direct order. The defence relied on the position that Inouye was a mere interpreter, not the person ordering and directing the tortures.

Haggan pointed to a number of the prosecution witnesses who received relatively mild treatment. For example, Inouye only slapped Madar. Haggan pointed out with some justification that "slapping is second nature to the Japanese." He said, "They do it to their own people and it is done in the Japanese Army ... Japanese soldiers who are slapped think nothing of it.... If the slapping of Madar is to be part of the charge against Inouye then every Japanese whoever came to China should be before this Court, or some Court as a war criminal."[22] It was a valid point and should have caused the judges to sit back and consider the ramifications. Japanese soldiers were regularly slapped, and it is not surprising that this was also meted out to their prisoners. However, the problem for Haggan was that Puddicombe had done his job, and there was a mass of reliable evidence that Inouye had gone well beyond the occasional slap. In numerous instances, he inflicted terrible pain on his victims over prolonged periods of time. The best Haggan could do was to remind the court about the occasion when Inouye offered to help Mary Power and assist her husband. He suggested that the accused was not a monster and hardly a major war criminal, for he "does not appear to me to be regarded as a violent and ruthless type. He may have delighted perhaps in a little influence and given to petty tyranny."[23]

After the addresses, the court adjourned at 4:40 p.m. The presiding officers returned with their verdict in less than an hour. The speed with which they decided a case that had taken up five days of evidence, lengthy arguments, and the consideration of Inouye's absent witnesses, is breathtaking. It seemed to reflect the likelihood that the officers had pretty well made up their minds early on. While Inouye was found guilty on all three charges, the court was not satisfied that there was sufficient proof he had killed the four persons named on the charge sheet. Colonel Stewart then asked if Inouye wished to speak on the question of the sentence. He deferred to Haggan who reminded the court of the realities of Japanese military discipline or, as he called it, "the true nature of the Japanese system, how little opportunity there is for one caught in the wheel to revolt against the machine" and how "he [Inouye] is a man caught up in a set of circumstances which he could not possibly control."[24]

In a mere fifteen minutes, the officers returned with their decision. It was perfunctory, yet its few words revealed a great deal about the authors:

> Inouye Kanao you have been found guilty of being concerned in may [sic] acts of ill-treatment. Some of these acts included such wanton and barbarous cruelty that it was a mere accident of fate whether the victims survived or not.
>
> Your culpability is greatly aggravated by the fact that you were the guest of the Dominion of Canada in your youth and there you received kindness and free education which should have impressed on your mind the decent ways of civilised people and made it impossible for you to be concerned, directly or indirectly, in such an outrage against humanity. By your barbaric acts you have destroyed your right to live, and the unanimous sentence of this Court, which is subject to confirmation, is that you will suffer death by hanging.[25]

It was a remarkable conclusion. Apparently, Inouye was far more accountable than the ordinary Japanese civilian due to his exposure to Western morality. While a level of barbarity could be expected in the average Japanese, Inouye had the benefit of contact with Christian ethics and therefore had to bear the full responsibility for his acts. Another factor adding to his culpability was his time spent as a "guest" in Canada. It would have been beyond the court's grasp to have considered that Inouye was actually a Canadian. Despite his birth in the country or the patriotic deeds of his father, he remained the "other," a mere "guest" who was only tarrying in Canada before going somewhere else. But the court found that even as a guest, Inouye should have been able to drop the wanton cruelty that supposedly marked his culture, for he had been exposed to the decent ways of civilized people. In his case, these efforts failed to make an impression and now he would pay the price.

It is a long-standing cliché that military justice is to justice as military music is to music. At Inouye's war crimes trial, there certainly seems to have been little consideration of issues such as his duty to obey or the deprivation of his right to call witnesses. Both were serious breaches of any notion of a fair trial. But most disturbingly, if sentences are supposed to be consistent and proportionate to the harm done, the death sentence was extraordinarily out of proportion to the other sentences being levied by other military courts. Indeed, Colonel Stewart's tribunal found that there was no proof that Inouye killed anyone, and there was little evidence that any of his subjects sustained permanent injuries. For example, a civilian interpreter attached to the Kempeitai at Kuala Lumpur was found guilty of a string of beatings and water tortures similar to those committed by Inouye. He was sentenced to five years in prison.[26] It was unusual for a defendant who had neither killed anyone nor caused permanent harm to be sentenced to die.

Inouye's conduct was certainly reprehensible, and there was ample evidence that he used his position to indulge in sadistic inclinations, yet the verdict demonstrated a remarkable lack of consistency. As subsequent cases would show, defendants such as Niimori Genichiro, who was directly responsible for the deaths of prisoners, received far less severe sentences. Inouye's case may have stood out due to his abuse of a woman, but for the most part, his actions were consistent with Japanese procedures. If every guard who slapped or harmed a prisoner must die, then the Allies better be prepared to execute hundreds of their Japanese captives.

It might have seemed a faint hope, but Inouye's last resort was a plea to the military high command in Singapore to reverse the decision. Both he and Haggan began to work on a draft shortly after the verdict.

8

DECISION ANNULLED

THE DEATH SENTENCE AGAINST THE "KAMLOOPS KID" WAS NOT BIG news in Canada. His former hometown newspaper, the *Kamloops Sentinel*, ran the headline "'Slap Happy Joe' to Die."[1] The newspaper was a bit vague on the facts and thought he was condemned for his part in atrocities at the Sham Shui Po camp. More accurately, they noted that older residents remembered a Japanese family of the name of Inouye whose father worked at the lumber mills and who moved to the coast after the Great War. There was subdued satisfaction in the *Sentinel* report that the "most sadistic of all camp officials"[2] would hang. The *Vancouver Sun* published a brief report of the sentence that Inouye would die for his actions under the headline "BC Born Jap must Die for Atrocities."[3] For the most part, the press across Canada ignored the proceedings at the Hong Kong trial and gave only a perfunctory account of the outcome. It was apparent that the public was far more interested in events in Europe than in Asia. The war crimes trial of S.S. general Kurt Meyer before a Canadian military tribunal was front page news in Canada through most of December 1945. Interest in Japanese war criminals was minimal.

Events concerning the Japanese in Canada were far more pressing and frequently the subject of public debate. Long before the end of the war in the Pacific, it was apparent that the Japanese Canadian community of British Columbia as it existed before the war was at an end. Their businesses and land were confiscated, their people dispersed. By 1944, it was apparent that many Japanese families were moving on to Ontario where, in addition to farming jobs, they could be employed in factories or trade. Many of those forced from the coast had set down new roots. One Montreal evacuee wrote to a friend in B.C., "As far as the Japanese returning back to Vancouver, I doubt very much they will. Most of us are making a new start in life."[4]

A headline in the *Vancouver Sun* said it all: "All Japanese Ordered Out of BC: East of the Rockies or Back to Japan."[5] In the case of Inouye's older sister Martha, her husband was Japanese-born and he particularly felt the animosity against his people. While Martha's husband wished to remain on the Pacific coast and then return to Japan once the war was over, she had other ideas. Government officials approached the family and asked if they would sign the documents to relocate after the war. Martha refused. She had known no other home than Canada and was willing to move east rather than agree to repatriation. The family moved to Chatham, Ontario, and began work at a dairy farm.[6]

While Inouye's war crimes trial was drawing to a close, a series of tragedies were playing out for many Japanese Canadians. On May 27, the *Toronto Star* reported on a party of repatriates who were bound to travel to Japan in a few days. One was an older man who served in the Canadian Army in the First World War. His possessions in B.C. were sold for a fraction of their value and he was relocated to the prairies. He told a reporter that repatriation was his only option since he could not go back to the West Coast because of the hostile attitude toward the Japanese. One family was broken apart — a mother, father, daughter, and youngest son were going back to Japan while the older sons remained. The returnees "sat in the rail car sobbing as they said goodbye to the three boys."[7] In February 1946, the Supreme Court of Canada upheld the legality of deportation but was divided on the question of deporting Nisei or unwilling dependents. Five ships would carry four thousand people, most of them Issei, back to war-torn Japan. However, there was a rising sense that this policy was profoundly unfair and should be halted. Many religious and labour organizations began to confront Prime Minister King that the deportation "was an assault on Canadian democracy and must not be allowed to occur."[8]

Little of this impacted Inouye, and it was unlikely that he heard or even knew about relocations or internments. In any event, he had enough of his own problems. Canadian Army interpreters Roy Ito and Fred Nogami commiserated with Inouye in the yard at Stanley Prison, where he was confined. He told them, "I'll get out of it. The death sentence is not fair!"[9] His sense of victimhood grew in succeeding weeks when he observed the results of other cases where those convicted of atrocities more heinous than his were given prison terms. He had an even greater inducement to survive because he was now a father. Roy Ito later recalled: "A woman said to be Inouye's pregnant wife lived alone in a dilapidated shack at Fort Stanley. Members of the War Crimes Investigation Unit took a collection and sent her powdered milk, diapers, blankets and other necessities. She gave birth to a healthy baby and was photographed dressed in a colourful kimono smilingly holding her child. I never knew what happened to her and the baby."[10]

Haggan went to work on the petition shortly after the court martial concluded. It would be as close as he could get to filing an appeal on Inouye's behalf, so he raised every possible irregularity that might catch a reviewing officer's attention. First, he pointed out how the accused wanted to call several witnesses. These persons might have provided a better understanding of what occurred, or at the very least, they might have bolstered Inouye's story that he was just an interpreter. Haggan further argued that the verdict was against the weight of the evidence in that Inouye had to obey direct orders. Several British officers confirmed the exacting standards of the Japanese military that made disobedience unthinkable. In answer to the third charge, that he tortured so many Hong Kong residents, Haggan went through the transcript of testimony and pointed out occasions when a few victims testified that Inouye's part was no greater than to obey orders and have them hung from a beam. He submitted that some evidence was pure fiction. For example, Inouye and Gonzalo Sang did not speak any common language, therefore there was no point for him to be present to interpret. Inouye witnessed Lam Sik being slapped and kicked by Moriyama but had not taken part. As for Ghilote, the most dramatic witness against the accused, Inouye maintained that he was a paid informer and that he was not tortured as he readily volunteered information. All the arrests were made based on Ghilote's information and he was the instigator of all that followed.

Haggan made no attempt to challenge the legality of convicting on the basis of torture since it was apparent that ill treatment was now internationally recognized as a war crime. It was also apparent that Japanese authorities used their position to inflict suffering on many, and as legal scholar Lutz Oette noted, "The treatment of civilians in occupied countries (during World War II) was frequently characterized by arbitrary brutality and racially motivated contempt fed by the ideologies of the occupiers."[11] Torture was now an established war crime, and, if proven, merited severe punishment. It was on the question of Inouye's origins that Haggan successfully distinguished his client's case from that of other alleged war criminals. Colonel Stewart pointed out that Inouye's conduct was far more reprehensible than would be a person from Japan without exposure to the enlightenment of Christian doctrine. It was a remarkable conclusion, and one without any foundation in law. A defendant was supposed to be judged on the basis of what they did, not on who they were. Haggan correctly pointed out that Inouye's place of origin was irrelevant and did not provide grounds for increasing the penalty. On a personal note, he added that since Inouye's arrest in September 1945, he had assisted Allied officers in interpreting the interrogations of several Japanese war criminals. The Allies were so hardpressed to locate persons who were fluent in both Japanese and English that Inouye's services were welcomed. Finally, in what seemed a last desperate roll of the dice, Haggan added that the military court had no jurisdiction in that Inouye was a Canadian and therefore not subject to a war crimes trial by the Allies. Due to the rush to judgment in May, Haggan did not have the opportunity to obtain his birth documents. He now had a photostat copy of Inouye's birth record that clearly showed he was born in Kamloops, British Columbia. Inouye claimed his right as a citizen: "and if tried for any offence at all I claim that I should be tried under Canadian Law by a competent civil court there." He signed the petition in a firm, round hand: "Kanao Inouye."[12]

After the filing of the petition on June 6, 1946, matters went into a state of hiatus. Paperwork had to flow through to the headquarters of ALFSEA in Singapore to be stamped in and considered. In the meantime, Inouye bided his time in Stanley Prison among the rest of the military and police staff who were waiting for their trials or repatriation. Inouye was gaining a reputation as a troublesome inmate. He began to pull tricks such as calling the cell block to attention even though no officer was approaching. Neither did he mask his anger at other inmates who he felt had caused all his troubles. He vowed that he would get out of the death sentence and settle scores with the Kempeitai staff who bullied him during the war. Sgt. Maj. Hayashi Sadataro recalled that Inouye resented once being disciplined by him. Inouye occupied the cell next to him, and he "used to tell me that he was going to take revenge on me, and he threatened me always."[13]

Major Puddicombe learned of the petition in early July 1946 and reported at length to the Canadian war crimes commander in Asia, Colonel Orr. In Puddicombe's mind, Inouye's assertion that he was a Canadian was highly questionable. He thought it likely that any native-born Japanese could obtain certification of Canadian birth as a ruse to stay in Canada. If Inouye was somehow able to use his alleged place of birth to avoid the consequences of his acts, Puddicombe mused that he might well be taken to Canada to face trial under the Treachery Act of 1940. The problem was that this statute did not mandate a death sentence, and in Puddicombe's opinion, Inouye "certainly deserves nothing less than hanging."[14] He was obviously concerned that the war criminal he invested such effort in getting convicted and sentenced to death might walk away free.

The trials he prosecuted after the Inouye case soured Puddicombe on the British approach toward punishing war criminals. Following the Inouye court martial, the next case handled by Puddicombe also concerned an interpreter, Niimori Genichiro,[15] who had learned English in Dayton, Ohio, and served as chief interpreter at Sham Shui Po since March 1942. Similar to the charge against Inouye, Niimori was accused of nursing a host of grievances against white people and using his position to exact revenge. Canadian prisoners in particular would be the subject of his unrelenting brutality. On one occasion, he hit a number of hospital patients so badly that one died by suicide rather than face his abuse. Affidavits filed by survivors of the Royal Regiment detailed how he beat Rifleman Doucett so badly that he never recovered and died not long after the event. The most serious charges against Niimori stemmed from his actions on board the *Lisbon Maru* when eighteen hundred British POWs were taken to forced labour in Japan. Torpedoed by an American submarine on October 1, 1942, the ship began to list and the prisoners were locked below decks in the hold. An officer begged Niimori to open the hold so the men could breathe and to send them water. Niimori suggested that they drink their own urine. A bucket of urine was the only relief offered to the trapped men.

As men tried to escape from the sinking ship, POWs could hear Niimori shouting to guards and firing on the swimmers. Those few who made it out were all captured. The naked, exhausted men were assembled on a wharf at Shanghai where they faced an infuriated Niimori, who marched among the survivors slashing them with a piece of wood. Later, Niimori bragged that there were no escapes since he locked the prisoners on the doomed ship. Compared to Inouye's "petty tyrannies," Niimori's unrestrained sadism had undoubtedly cost the lives of many men. But the same British officers — Stewart, Ormsby, and Kaul — who made up No. 7 War Crimes Court and heard Inouye's case sentenced Niimori to only fifteen years in jail. Upon hearing the sentence, Niimori, obviously thinking he had a date with the hangman, jumped up, embraced his lawyers, and bowed repeatedly to the Court.

George Puddicombe was beyond himself with rage and disbelief. He wrote to Colonel Orr that "if ever I am found guilty of being an accessory to the murder of 900 odd. [*sic*] human beings, I hope I may be sentenced by No. 7 War Crimes Court."[16] The absurdly lenient sentence levied on Niimori caused Puddicombe to question his role in the proceedings. He asked Orr if he had failed somehow to fully present the prosecution's case. If so, perhaps he should be relieved from presenting the major case that was scheduled in a few days against the Sham Shui Po camp commandant Tokunaga Isao, Dr. Saito Shunkichi, and three others. With confidence in Puddicombe's

abilities, Orr left him in charge of the "Camp case," one of the most important and, for once, publicized hearings handled by a Canadian prosecutor in
Hong Kong.

In mid-May 1946, long before the trial and only a few days after the
Inouye verdict, Puddicombe conducted some investigation of his own, which
substantially bolstered the case against Tokunaga and Saito. Tokunaga was
responsible for Sham Shui Po for most of the stay by the Canadians. One
officer recalled that Tokunaga once told them that international rules did
not apply there, and that "there was only one law in the world and that was
the law of the Imperial Japanese Army."[17] Both Tokunaga and the guards
pilfered Red Cross parcels intended for the POWs and sold them on the
black market. Under his direction, sick and fit men alike were sent off for
fifteen-hour shifts of heavy labour rebuilding the Kai Tak Airport. In addition to routine slappings, guards also gave out prolonged beatings that left
men unconscious, and many of these attacks were carried out in full view
of the commandant's office. Not only was he responsible for exploiting the
POWs' labour, Tokunaga was also indifferent to their conditions. Men were
crammed into huts and left exposed to wind and rain. During the charade
of a Red Cross inspection, one Canadian soldier, Private Barnett, had the
courage to call out, "We are being starved."[18] He was subsequently taken out
and savagely beaten. Given the context of his surroundings, Kanao Inouye
was not unique. In Tokunaga's camp, to act with a measure of humanity
would have been the exception.

The case against Dr. Saito was based on his mishandling of the diphtheria outbreak and his refusal to supply medicines, which might have saved
many of the Canadians who died of the disease. Diphtheria was treatable,
and all it required was to identify the infected, isolate them, and treat them
with serum. But at the Bowen Road Hospital, serum was not being provided.
Those medical orderlies who were daring enough to get some serum on the
black market managed to save a few of their comrades. One POW recorded
that at the height of the outbreak, a senior Japanese medical officer toured
the camp and almost immediately the serum was provided, which Saito had
insisted was unavailable. In most cases, Saito was content to withhold care.
In Puddicombe's dramatic closing remarks, he termed Saito's responsibility

for the death of a diphtheria patient as "no less than if he had grasped the man by the throat and choked him to death."[19]

By far the most explosive evidence presented at the Camp case was the outright murder of four Canadians in August 1942. On August 21, 1942, Sgt. John Payne, Lt. Cpl. George Berzenski, and Pvts. John Adams and Percy Ellis engineered an escape from the North Point camp. Climbing over the roof, the men stole a sampan and attempted to cross the harbour to the mainland. They were never seen again. Tokunaga's first story, that they tried to sneak through the fence and were shot, was contradicted by all available evidence and soon discarded. He then said that they were caught and shot during an escape, but Chinese witnesses recalled the POWs being taken to the headquarters, where they were beaten by soldiers and then brought to the King's Park football field. On June 26, 1946, a month after the conclusion of Inouye's case, Puddicombe took Tokunaga, Saito, and every other Japanese prisoner who was present at the arrest of the four Canadians to the football field. They told Puddicombe that they thought the Canadians were buried elsewhere. He suspected that they were lying and insisted that the four were buried somewhere in King's Park. Puddicombe told Tokunaga, Saito, and several other accused that they had five minutes to point out the grave, and if they did not, they were going to start digging and keep on digging until the remains were found. It was a bluff, but it worked. Saito admitted that the men had been executed and pointed out where the bodies were buried.

Inouye would be called on to play a small role in the Camp case. One of the minor characters among the five accused, Tsutada "Stodda" Itsudo, was an interpreter like Inouye. Born in Singapore and therefore a British subject, he spoke flawless English. And much like Inouye, he had earned a reputation for brutality toward the POWs. One witness recalled how Stodda used a wooden scabbard to strike them and had a habit of slapping people across the face with both hands. According to a Major Boxer, Stodda was "the worst type of person of any nationality whom he had ever met." Even the affidavit of the Canadian officer Frank Power filed at the Inouye trial noted that Stodda seemed to be the brain behind the other guards. The purpose of linking Stodda to the Tokunaga/Saito proceedings was to show how the senior camp administrators tolerated and even encouraged the abuse and humiliation of prisoners. Inouye was called by the defence to try to establish that his colleague Stodda's conduct was not as bad as all that. Inouye stated that he only witnessed Stodda strike a Dutch officer twice, and it was their superior, Lieutenant Wada, who ordered several other Dutch sailors slapped for hiding a shortwave radio. Though Stodda was convicted, he was sentenced to only two years in prison. Inouye must have been left wondering why he was denied such leniency.

For most of December 1946, the *South China Morning Post* reported details of the Camp case on its front page.[20] In his defence, Tokunaga tried to shift the blame to his superiors, but it was apparent that troops under his direct command had murdered the four Canadians and done what they could to hide the deed. Both Tokunaga and Saito were sentenced to death. A review of their cases by British headquarters in Singapore did not result in any changes. There was a suggestion that perhaps Saito's sentence was too severe, and he received support from British doctors who thought there were problems getting medical supplies and that the shortage was not entirely his fault. The acting commander of the British land forces in Hong Kong was given the final word. Brigadier Rogers upheld the guilty verdicts, but in an unexpected turn, commuted the death sentences of both Tokunaga and Saito — the former to life in prison, the latter to twenty years. Almost out of embarrassment, word of the commutation was not passed on directly to the Canadians. When it was finally sent out, it was in a one-line communiqué.

As historian Mark Sweeney observed, "Although Puddicombe had secured the conviction and provided the lion's share of the evidence, Canadian officials had no say in the ultimate fate of war criminals — and did not even warrant a clear explanation."[21] This time the military trials in Hong Kong caught the Canadian public's attention but not in a favourable way. Veteran groups condemned this misplaced mercy and what appeared to be British indifference to the deaths of their Canadian comrades. Months after the fact, when Puddicombe was back in Canada and could speak freely as a civilian, he told a reporter from the *Montreal Standard* that evidence he presented had shown that Tokunago and Saito were responsible for the deaths of 125 Canadian POWs. "How many men does a man have to kill to be hanged?" he asked.[22]

In the meantime, Orr and Puddicombe passed messages debating the nature of Inouye's nationality. In July, Puddicombe speculated that even if Inouye was born in Canada — a fact that he doubted — he could have become a naturalized citizen of Japan. If he was conscripted by the Japanese military and made no objection, then "would this not raise the presumption *juris tantum* that he was Japanese?"[23] Orr responded some time later that Inouye had indeed been conscripted as if he was a Japanese national. He forwarded a press clipping about a native-born American serving in the Japanese military who was tried for war crimes before an Australian panel. That case had caused no difficulties. Moreover, Arthur Rance had sworn that in October 1942 while travelling with Inouye on the Star Ferry boat to Sham Shui Po, Inouye confided to him that he was actually born in Tokyo and was taken to Canada at the age of two. The only conclusion Orr and Puddicombe could reach was that the nationality question was a thorny one and merely establishing the place of birth did not resolve it.[24]

On November 14, 1946, after a wait of more than five months, the British military headquarters in Singapore finally released their decision. The Canadian detachment in Japan had obtained evidence that Inouye was indeed born in Canada and forwarded it to ALFSEA for consideration. The reviewing officer, Col. F.C.A. Kerin, accepted Inouye's proof of citizenship and found that on the basis of his Canadian birth, he was a Canadian citizen and therefore a British subject. This was the only factor he considered. He then concluded that he was beyond the jurisdiction of the war crimes courts and that his trial was invalid. As a matter of practice, only Japanese personnel or their Formosan and Korean auxiliaries were tried for war crimes. But on the face of it, the statute included any persons who committed war crimes against the Allies. The provisions of the Royal Warrant applied to captured enemy personnel, and there was no legal basis why a British subject serving in the Japanese Army should be exempt from the regulations.

Nevertheless, the ALFSEA legal authorities had spoken. The result was that Inouye's court martial was a nullity and he was in the position of not having been tried at all. Colonel Kerin gratuitously added that he could still be tried by the civil authorities in Hong Kong, "or he might be returned to Canada for trial there."[25] This was a matter to be decided by the civilian governments of Hong Kong or Canada, but in either case, he must be released from British military custody. There was always the possibility that since Inouye was not subject to any war crimes charges, he might simply walk out of prison a free man.

9

TREASON?

ONE PERSON WAS DETERMINED THAT THIS WOULD NEVER HAPPEN. IN the following weeks, Oscar Orr would do everything possible to keep Inouye in custody. He wrote to the Department of National Defence in Ottawa on October 14, 1946, to warn them that a petition to exonerate Inouye was pending. This caused reverberations in Ottawa as various departments once again debated what to do with Inouye. Army deputy minister Ross contacted External Affairs on November 6, and warned them that "there would appear to be a distinct possibility that Kanao Inouye might be released from custody, with the further possibility that he might then disappear entirely."[1] Ross urged the External Affairs Department to press authorities in Hong Kong to hold him as long as possible.

The main fear was that somehow Inouye might end up in Canada and become an even greater headache for officialdom. National Defence passed the ball to External Affairs, which, in turn, held that there was nothing to be done beyond ensuring that he remained in custody since the case was still undetermined. M.H. Wershof, the clerk for the undersecretary of state for External Affairs, left it to the Canadian mission in Tokyo to communicate with authorities in Hong Kong to ensure that Inouye would be held for at least another thirty days. For his part, Wershof was hesitant to bring the Inouye situation before Cabinet again and felt that nothing was to be done unless there was no choice but to bring him back to Canada. Although the case so far attracted negligible publicity in Canada, it was possible that Canadian POW groups would want to see retribution applied to the infamous "Kamloops Kid." But Hong Kong civilians, who had suffered far more at his hands, also wanted justice. The problem was that the military court indicated that there was no proof that Inouye had ever killed anyone. What was to be done with him? It was Oscar Orr who came up with a suggestion that satisfied the diplomats as well as the civil servants of Hong Kong. It would also be a very cold-blooded solution to the Inouye problem.

On October 29, 1946, Orr wrote to Puddicombe that perhaps the best way to proceed was to charge Inouye with high treason. In that manner, he could be tried before a Hong Kong jury with offences committed against their friends and relatives. Orr followed the original war crimes trial closely: "My impression is that the Canadian case of relying on evidence of prisoners of war, would be very trifling indeed compared to the case you presented dealing with his conduct in the gendarmerie."[2] Orr also consulted with E.H. Norman, the head of Canada's mission in Japan and the country's diplomatic head in Asia. Norman enthusiastically seized on this course of action and wrote to his British counterpart in Tokyo, Alvary Gascoigne, requesting that Inouye stay in custody. Norman went on to describe his conversation with Orr in which the colonel urged that Inouye be tried for treason by a civil court in Hong Kong, as "the serious case against Inouye comes from his treatment of civilians interned in Hong Kong," rather than forwarding him to Canada, which had "a weaker case since Inouye's behavior towards Canadian prisoners of war is a comparatively minor aspect of the charges against him."[3] This approach also meant that he would be tried for an offence that carried the death penalty.

•

Kanao Inouye was not the only Canadian who could have been charged with treason after the Second World War. Three members of the Essex Scottish

Regiment were accused of joining the German military or supplying the Germans with valuable information. All three soldiers were captured after the Dieppe raid in August 1942, and subjected to periodic Nazi indoctrination. One of the prisoners, Edwin Walker, of Riverside, Ontario, was one of the first members and organizers of the tiny, quixotic "British Free Corps," the only English-speaking unit in the German army during the Second World War. An enthusiastic volunteer, Walker designed the Corps flag and tried to recruit others. Significantly, Walker was not charged with treason but was court-martialed for having aided and abetted the enemy. The Canadian Army seemed relieved to give him a dishonourable discharge and a few years in prison.

On the other hand, based on the evidence from the war crimes trial, authorities knew about Inouye's wartime service and that he was forced into a civilian interpreter's job. Even when he tried to refuse the position due to his chest condition, the honour of serving the emperor was pressed upon him. It was true that in June 1944, he volunteered to work for the police, but it was apparent from the circumstances that this was the only way he could reunite with his wife. He did not appear to have been very enthusiastic about the Kempeitai and left when he could in early 1945. If he was a traitor, he appeared to be a most reluctant one. The prospect of holding onto him for a future trial seemed dim. Alvary Gascoigne responded to E.H. Norman in Tokyo that perhaps the British might wash their hands of Inouye entirely since it was always possible that he could be tried for treason in Canada. On November 25, Norman warned External Affairs that "in any case, the eventuality of release [of Inouye] both by military and Civil Authorities in Hong Kong should be considered."[4]

On November 15, 1946, the day after the notice that Inouye's conviction would be quashed, Gascoigne wrote from Tokyo to Hong Kong's governor, Sir Mark Young, to pass along the Canadian proposal about holding him liable for treason. Puddicombe sent a telegram to Orr on November 25, and they were now confident that Inouye would be held at least for a while in the colony. But as of yet, there was no decision as to whether he would be charged with treason or under the Treachery Act. If it was the latter, the maximum sentence would be life in prison. Puddicombe also took further steps to prod local authorities into action. He approached A. Lonsdale, the chief Crown prosecutor in the colony, to explore the viability of a treason charge. He responded to Puddicombe that Inouye had claimed British nationality and that it would be difficult for him to resile from this position. However, if he came up with a valid declaration renouncing British citizenship made before the war, the treason charge would fail. Furthermore, if he was found to be a Japanese, he could not be extradited to Canada as it would not appear that he had broken any Canadian law.[5] Canadian involvement in the case of Kanao Inouye became minimal and the primary initiative lay with the Hong Kong authorities. On November 27, 1946, the *Hongkong Telegraph* reported that Inouye was hurriedly taken before Mr. Sainsbury at the Central Magistracy and charged with treason.

Behind the scenes, Crown lawyers were far from convinced that they had enough evidence to prove treason. Orr was still fuming at ALFSEA's quashing of the war crimes verdict. In his opinion, just because Inouye was born in Canada did not mean that he was necessarily a Canadian. In a lengthy report to Puddicombe on December 5, he much regretted the snap judgment based on incomplete evidence of the British officers that Inouye was British.[6] Furthermore, he questioned whether the deciding panel contained any qualified member of the bar and doubted that they had any reasonable grounds for their opinion. The B.C. Vital Statistics Department was far from an unimpeachable source. Moreover, they also had proof that in February 1918, Inouye's father registered Kanao's birth with the Japanese Consul in Vancouver. Of course, this was impossible since Tadashi was thousands of miles away at war in France. The only explanation is that Mikuma had taken on the task of seeing the consul. It is likely she explained the situation that her husband might never return and she wanted to secure her son's place in the homeland by registering him in his father's family register with the proper Japanese authorities.

On this issue, Colonel Orr made some inquiries with E.H. Norman, who was born in Nagano and raised in Japan. Familiar with Japanese customs and traditions, Norman had written insightful books on the Japanese government in the 1930s. As a member of Canada's mission to Tokyo he was interned in 1941. As head of the mission, he caught the eye of the Supreme

Commander of the Allied Powers, General MacArthur, who appreciated Norman's keen understanding of the nation the general now governed. Norman was also an invaluable linchpin between the military and diplomatic staffs on dealing with the Inouye question. Orr reported the following: "Dr. Norman advises that the registration of births in the family register is an important part of the organization of Japanese life and would normally be done immediately after birth. Non-registration of a child would place the child under a most severe handicap in later life."[7] Therefore, under Japanese law, Inouye was registered as a citizen in their country.

There was another aspect of Inouye's career that had escaped examination until now. Orr talked with Sergeant Rance, the Japanese-speaking POW who was helping the Canadian staff with the Japan cases and previously developed a rapport with Inouye while in the POW camp. According to Rance, Inouye told him that after 1936, he served with the Imperial Japanese Army in China, was wounded, and was convalescing in Japan when Pearl Harbor was bombed. Due to his previous military service, he was "a somewhat senior brand of interpreter"[8] in Hong Kong. This was the first notice the Canadians had that Inouye had sworn allegiance to Japan's emperor, served in his army, and left behind any allegiance to Canada. In an opinion, that should have had significant consequences at any subsequent treason trial. Orr concluded that "if a man can abandon his previous allegiance by his own acts and declarations I think that this man has gone about as far in indicating his intention as any reasonable law would require of him."[9]

Whether or not Inouye formally renounced his Canadian citizenship was an open question. Once again, Orr put this issue to Dr. Norman, who informed him that some Japanese citizens formally abandoned foreign nationalities, but "these declarations were regarded as quite confidential and in other cases it has been very difficult to secure information regarding such action by individuals."[10] Such a declaration had to be filed with the British Home Office, and Orr advised that he would make inquiries with London. The most Canada could do at this point was to hire a Hong Kong solicitor to keep a watching brief on the proceedings. After reviewing Norman's advice, Orr concluded that "the above does not settle anything, but it does indicate that there is a great deal more to this case than a long range decision to the effect that a birth certificate proves citizenship," and further, that "a decision involving the life of a man on the one hand and the interests of a great country on the other should be made only after deep consideration of all relevant factors, plus notice to interested persons."[11] The prosecution was forewarned that a treason charge based on Inouye being a Canadian citizen might not be as formidable as they previously thought.

A week later, Orr made his formal report to National Defence in Ottawa. He complained that ALFSEA had left everything in disorder by precipitously ruling that Inouye was a Canadian citizen. British policies on citizenship certainly seemed to lack any consistency. He noted the case of Stodda, the interpreter who had benefitted from Inouye's testimony. Stodda was born in the British territory of Singapore, but since his birth was registered at the Japanese consulate, he was therefore considered Japanese.[12] Why should not the same principle be applied to Inouye?

Despite Orr's grumbling, the ALFSEA decision to annul the guilty verdict was made and the military hierarchy was not about to admit that it was fallible. Moreover, the Canadians were content, for the moment, to let matters play out in Hong Kong. Once it was apparent that the civil authorities would proceed with a treason charge, Puddicombe wrote to Orr that "our [Canadian] interest is small. The great complaint is about his conduct when he joined the gendarmerie." He also believed that the prosecution was in good hands: "Mr. Lonsdale thinks that the chances of establishing himself as a Japanese, in the face of his signed petition for release, is poor. He [Inouye] is going to make a good try, though."[13] Perhaps too good a try. By December 1946, messages were still going back and forth between deputy ministers of Ottawa ministries considering the possibility that Inouye might be acquitted of the treason charge by reason of his adopted Japanese nationality. External Affairs suggested that if the Hong Kong authorities were about to release him, then the case should again be brought before the Cabinet. A few days later, the deputy minister of justice, F.P. Varcoe, intervened in the debate and quashed any further discussion: "Pending the outcome of these proceedings, no action should be taken to bring this man to Canada for trial."[14]

During this interval, Inouye continued to make himself useful to his captors. In January 1947, he appeared as a prosecution witness at the trial of the Kempeitai commander Noma Kennosuke, who was charged with numerous counts of torture and executions without trial of suspects. At the end of September 1944, a prisoner, Gak Tai Ho, had escaped from prison with his girlfriend, Tai Koon-you. Both were caught and allowed a parting kiss before they were summarily shot at Noma's command. Inouye swore that he saw and read Noma's order to execute the couple. When asked whether he could read Japanese, Inouye replied, "I can read a little, enough to know characters." Noma was convicted and executed in 1947. In cross-examination, Inouye was questioned about his nationality. He replied that he was Japanese. The defence then asked him about his military service in Manchuria, but he declined to answer since he maintained that it might prejudice him in his upcoming trial.[15] Surprisingly, there appeared to be details about Inouye's background that he kept well hidden, for he had previously inferred that between 1936 and 1940, his pursuits were academic, not military. If he went through great lengths to fabricate a story about his congenial life in Canada, what other parts of his life story had he omitted or obscured?

In the meantime, Governor Young wanted more background information from ALFSEA on why they dismissed Inouye's military conviction. There did not seem to be any point in laying more charges if they were a dead end. The Canadian birth certificate was produced, and, once the authorities were satisfied that Inouye was likely a British subject, matters gained momentum. At the end of February 1947, Inouye was again brought before Magistrate Sainsbury to answer for twenty-eight counts of high treason arising from of his acts as a Kempeitai interpreter between June 1, 1944, and March 31, 1945. The Hong Kong English-language newspapers — who adopted the Canadian nickname and routinely referred to the accused as "Slap Happy Inouye"— covered all aspects of the case. Even if Inouye's fate was of little interest in Canada, Hong Kong residents were fascinated by the stories of torture being related daily from the witness stand. The exclusive question for the magistrate at this preliminary stage was whether Inouye should be committed for trial. The case for the prosecution was made all the easier when Inouye pleaded poverty and was not represented by a lawyer.

Over three days, prosecutor Lonsdale sent thirty-one witnesses to the stand to substantiate the charges. Many of them, such as Mary Power and Alfred Guest, had already appeared in the war crimes trial. Several more witnesses came forward, all of them Hong Kong residents, who testified that they were the victims of beatings or torture by Inouye.[16] All the charges dealt with his alleged mistreatment of Hong Kong residents, and none involved Canadian POWs. On March 18, Inouye was arraigned under the Treason Act of 1351 and he pleaded not guilty to all the accusations.

Kanao Inouye was about to tried for one of the most unusual and antiquated offences still on the English statute books. The Treason Act of 1351 was enacted during the reign of King Edward III. It provided that a subject could be convicted of high treason if he planned the death of the king, the king's heir, or if he had sex with the king's unmarried eldest daughter or the wife of the king's eldest son. Royal bloodlines had to be protected, and to violate them raised questions as to the divine right of the heir. Such a crime went to the heart of the sovereign's right to rule and could only be punished by death. At its core, the offence was one of betrayal, of being untrue to the king by taking up arms against him or threatening his right to rule. The Treason Act was a peculiar medieval relic to invoke in an age of atomic warfare in a case concerning an obscure interpreter in a colony half a world away from England. For that matter, the statute under which Kanao Inouye was charged was not even in English. Written in Norman French, the Treason Act made it punishable for a person *soit aherdant as enemys* [adhering to the enemies of the King] and *donant a eux eid ou confort* [giving them aid and comfort] to be put to death by the slow, agonizing method of being drawn and quartered.[17] In succeeding centuries, this was reduced to simple hanging.

From time to time, the Treason Act had been applied in colonial Canada. During the War of 1812, a group of Upper Canadian settlers who retained sympathies with the U.S. were seized while raiding their former neighbours. At the subsequent treason trial in the town of Ancaster in 1814, the Court dealt with the outlaws including the two Hartwell brothers who — despite swearing loyalty to the Crown to get a land grant in the colony — joined the American militia when war broke out. While their act was technically treasonous, the Hartwells felt that they were Americans at heart and joined the military force of their country. They were imprisoned but not executed. The same mercy was not applied to the irregulars who torched the country-side — eight of them were hanged.[18] The lesson was that as far back as 1814, Canadian authorities recognized that there were different levels of treason. They showed leniency toward subjects who served a country to which they retained some form of allegiance, but there was no mercy for those who terrorized their former neighbours. It was not the act of disloyalty that mattered, but what the person committed while disloyal. Could Inouye claim this lenience — that he was only serving his real country — or was his conduct similar to the more obnoxious irregulars?

During the rebellion in Upper and Lower Canada in 1837–38, treason charges were again levied against those who fought against the Crown. In Upper Canada (later Ontario), of the nearly 150 men who had risen in arms in 1837, only twelve were brought to trial, and only two of those were hanged for treason. Political expediency outweighed strict legal requirements for "legal and political considerations went hand-in-hand and were coordinated, with an eye to the delicate balance of retribution and preservation of the political status quo."[19] Even in that period, authorities appreciated that treason was a highly political matter and that the death penalty should be applied selectively. These considerations were of no use to Inouye since he did not represent a community and could call on no political sympathies.

The full weight of the law had fallen on another Canadian. After the suppression of the Northwest Rebellion in 1885, Louis Riel, the mystic leader of the Métis, was charged with high treason. An alternative charge of treason-felony was available, but prosecutors singled out Riel for high treason, which carried the death penalty. Even though there was conflicting evidence at Riel's trial in 1885 regarding his sanity and citizenship, he was sentenced to hang. This created a national uproar and several of his partisans, particularly in Quebec, argued that treason was a political indictment and that civilized nations no longer punished dissent with death. The government was unmoved, and Riel was executed on November 16, 1885.[20]

At the end of the Second World War, a parade of celebrities was tried for treason. Robert Brasillach, a French journalist, was prosecuted for the crime of "intelligence with the enemy."[21] An avid fascist and anti-Semite, Brasillach wrote propaganda for the Vichy government to justify collaboration with the Nazis; however odious his writings, he did not kill anyone. Nevertheless, he was convicted and executed. When Ezra Pound, the American poet, was flown to Washington for his treason trial in November 1945, his guilt seemed certain. An advocate for Mussolini's regime, Pound was known to have broadcast discouraging messages to American GIs in Italy. In order to verify these broadcasts, American prosecutors needed two witnesses, but the radio station staff who taped Pound's broadcasts did not speak or understand English. It seemed that laying a charge for treason was much easier than establishing it. Faced with these difficulties, the treason charges were dropped, and psychiatric evidence was put forward to prove that Pound was insane and unfit to stand trial.[22]

Even more insurmountable difficulties arose at the treason trial of what may have been one of the most flamboyant postwar defendants, William Joyce. American-born and Irish-raised, Joyce served in the British Union of Fascists during the 1930s and was one of their principal orators and street brawlers. Joyce moved to Germany before the outbreak of war; his program, "Germany Calling!" became the principal propaganda outlet aimed at the British public that also featured some of the latest American swing music. Calling himself "Lord Haw-Haw," Joyce became a major public persona disparaging the British war effort and predicting an eventual German victory. At one point, his audience was estimated to be significantly larger than that of the stodgy BBC.

At his 1945 treason trial, Joyce argued that he owed no allegiance to the king since he was American-born and had never taken out British citizenship, and his alleged treasonous activities were conducted outside the country. Both were powerful arguments militating against guilt. Nevertheless, in the determination to punish the enemy, Joyce was convicted on the basis of once falsely attesting on a passport application that he was British. Historian A.J.P. Taylor observed that Joyce thereby became the only person ever executed for having lied on a passport application. Not long after Joyce's execution, legal scholars began to question the propriety of the decision. An accused could only betray a country if they were a citizen of that country. Lord Haw-Haw's case and the question of loyalty would be raised during the Inouye treason trial, but the outcome of Joyce's case might have been a warning that the postwar courts would not be overly concerned with fine legal distinctions.[23]

All of these treason trials were directed against high-profile celebrity figures who defied their countries and supported the enemy during the life and death struggle of war. Their trials and punishments served a political purpose in demonstrating the consequences of disloyalty. In contrast, Kanao Inouye was a nonentity whose crimes were committed in an area far removed from the major action, which were strictly a matter of local concern and were publicized for the most part only in Hong Kong. Moreover, it was difficult to understand how Inouye's conduct, no matter how reprehensible, actually threatened the rule of King George VI. Nevertheless, the authorities chose to stake everything on the charge of disloyalty.

Even though they remained in the background, Orr and Puddicombe achieved their desired result. Inouye now faced a charge for which, if convicted, the death penalty was likely. It was a result to be fervently desired, at least by George Puddicombe. As he had written to his superior the previous July, Inouye "certainly deserves nothing less than hanging."[24]

10

DEFENCE GAMBLE

PRESIDING OVER THE TREASON TRIAL WOULD BE SIR HENRY BLACKALL, an Irish aristocrat and a proconsul of the British Empire. A senior criminal prosecutor in Africa since 1919, he steadily worked his way up the imperial ladder until he was made chief justice of Trinidad and Tobago in 1943. His appointment as chief justice of Hong Kong in 1946 was only another way station in a series of distinguished appointments. Since any trial in which a life was at stake required legal representation, the government hired Charles Loseby to work on Inouye's defence. Loseby came from a grittier background than Blackall. Before the First World War, he taught school, studied law, and was called to the bar just as the war broke out. Gassed at the battle of Ypres in 1915, he went back to the law after the war and briefly served in Parliament. In 1946, he decided to try his luck in Hong Kong. His motives for doing so are obscure, but first-rate English counsel drawing comfortable fees did not relocate to what was considered a colonial backwater. Following the British tradition, Loseby spoke in court, while the solicitor H.K. Woo would assist him with paperwork and research. The charges would be prosecuted by Hong Kong's senior Crown counsel, A. Lonsdale, assisted by two police inspectors. Except for the solicitor, Woo, it is unlikely that any of these court officers were fluent in Cantonese.

The jurors who would decide Inouye's fate stood in marked contrast to these English gentlemen. Nam Sen Koo, Tsang Wah Shin, and Pak Lien Wong were local Chinese citizens, while the other four jurors were Hong Kong residents from English backgrounds. All of them undoubtedly recalled the times only a few months past when Kempeitai officers strutted through their streets and 69 Kimberley Road was a feared address. All of them, English or Chinese, had endured the suffocating shroud of the Japanese occupation for almost four years. Roy Ito, the Canadian army interpreter who had become a partisan on Inouye's behalf, felt that it was a jury of "whites and Chinese, representing the community which hated the Japanese Canadian."[1] According to Ito, Inouye would not be tried by a jury of his peers, but by a jury of his enemies.

For his part, Inouye seemed to be undergoing a change in attitude and was turning a new leaf regarding his fellow prisoners. During the Camp case of Colonel Tokunaga and Dr. Saito, Inouye was called on to act as a defence witness on behalf of his fellow interpreter, Tsutada Itsuo. Refusing to speak English, Inouye gave all his testimony in Japanese. Not only was he now assisting his former comrades, by early 1947 there were unusual reports that Inouye was re-inventing his past. In February, Puddicombe informed Orr that Inouye was now refusing to speak English. Even when his former counsel, Haggan, visited him, Inouye declined to address him except through a Japanese interpreter. Puddicombe also found out that "he [Inouye] appeared in Noma's case and pronounced himself a Jap. He appeared in the Camp case [Tokunaga] and elected to speak Japanese."[2] It seemed that Inouye was in the midst of a metamorphosis and that an entirely different persona from the previous year was about to emerge.

At least this time Inouye was to be tried in a proper courtroom. The Ordinary Criminal Session of the Supreme Court of Hong Kong sat in the stately Supreme Court building. Surrounded by classical columns, the Supreme Court was a jewel in Victoria City and since 1912, it was a centrepiece of the colonial administration. During the Japanese occupation, it had been the residence for senior Kempeitai staff and was used in their

Supreme Court building, Victoria City, Hong Kong, 1946–47.

operations. It was an irony that the quiet, orderly courtrooms where trials were being conducted had recently been the site of hideous interrogations and tortures. When the trial began on Tuesday, April 15, 1947, defence counsel Charles Loseby wasted no time in rising to his feet and raising an objection to the charge of twenty-seven overt acts of high treason. The facts as alleged were far too vague to permit the accused to mount a defence. He reasoned that any person charged with so serious an offence had a right to know exactly what facts were being alleged. Significantly, he added a reference to the recently hanged William Joyce and demanded that the Crown prosecution state its case whether they felt that Inouye was a British subject, or whether he was an alien who owed allegiance on other grounds. The issue of Inouye's nationality probably arose earlier than the prosecution antici-pated, but Lonsdale was nonetheless prepared to respond. He admitted that in the *Joyce* case, the Crown was forced to seek an amendment when it surfaced that the accused was not born a British subject; however, that was not the case for Inouye as it was apparent that he was born in Canada, a country that made him a British subject.[3] Loseby at least boxed in the prosecution on this issue, and the Crown would have to rely solely on the fact of Inouye's Canadian birth to prove treason. The court then adjourned as Sir Henry was invited to take part in an investiture at the governor's mansion, an occasion that trumped any court proceedings.

While this was an entirely new trial under a fresh set of charges, what had happened at Inouye's war crimes trial almost a year ago was not far from mind. When the chief justice returned from the lofty proceedings at Government House, he was confronted by two of the principal figures from the previous case. Maj. George Puddicombe took the witness stand and confirmed that his staff had procured Inouye's birth certificate confirming that while his parents came from Tokyo, he was born in Kamloops, British Columbia, in 1916. He was followed by Inouye's former defence counsel, the newly promoted Capt. John Haggan, who identified the petition against the conviction and Inouye's insistence at the time that he was a Canadian: "My impression was that he was aware of his nationality. He always claimed to be a Canadian." However, Inouye never mentioned to Haggan that his birth was also registered at the Japanese Consulate in Vancouver. A subsequent search conducted by the Canadian War Crimes Branch in Japan uncovered this document, but this was not the only new document the defence wished to bring forward.

Loseby rose and notified the judge that the defence was embarrassed by the absence of certain documents they had been trying to get from Japan. He confirmed to the judge that he required proof relating to the registration of Inouye's residency in Japan as well as his military record in the Japanese Army. They would all prove to be crucial to the defence in order to establish Inouye's nationality. But Loseby was ambivalent about their necessity, and he agreed that the trial could proceed without them. It seemed that his commitment toward mounting a vigorous defence was questionable.

It was not until the following morning that the extent of the evidence against the accused and the nature of his defence was revealed. The foundation of the prosecution would be laid by two Japanese witnesses. Matsuda Kenichiro served with Inouye as a military translator in 1942 and recalled Inouye returning to Hong Kong in 1944 in search of work. Nothing was available for him at the POW camps, but he did get a job with the police. He was followed by Maj. Shiozawa Kunio, an army officer and the head of the Tokko political affairs department of the Kempeitai. He remembered Inouye arriving in Hong Kong without a passport and being liable to be deported back to Japan. Inouye begged Shiozawa for a job with the police handling translations. Shiozawa took him on in the summer of 1944 but recalled that Inouye only stayed until February 1945.[4] The Tokko branch had been reorganized, and interpreters were no longer required. As transportation was impossible, Inouye would have to remain in Hong Kong. Shiozawa did not know the facts behind Inouye's departure, other than hearing that he was dissatisfied with the pay. The point was made — whatever his reasons, Inouye had volunteered to work for the Kempeitai.

The rest of the day's witnesses largely repeated the evidence from the war crimes trial. Rampal Ghilote went over the story of being approached by the police at the Peninsula Hotel. According to him, he said that he could be of no help and was sent home. A few days later, he was arrested and interrogated. The water torture was applied to him three times, and on each occasion, Inouye checked his pulse. After the third treatment, Ghilote confessed that he had once gone to John Power's house to listen to war news on his radio. Ghilote was handcuffed and the police raided Power's home. When they only discovered a licensed radio, Inouye had turned on him and said, "You fool, why have you brought us here?"[5] Taken back to 69 Kimberley Road, Ghilote was tortured for hours, with Inouye making periodic demands that he confess. Burned and left hanging for hours, Ghilote eventually said whatever came into his head and was released from torture. Inouye continued to visit him in his cell and demand that he confess, but Ghilote denied everything.

There might have been some question that Ghilote was actually an informer and was being punished for having given bad information; however, this version would never be tested, for as soon as Ghilote finished testifying in chief, Loseby stood and announced that he would not cross-examine him or, for that matter, any of the Crown witnesses. The defence was based exclusively on their position that Inouye owed his sole allegiance to the emperor of Japan, that he owed no duty to the king of England but was obliged to fight him and his soldiers. Loseby went on to explain that this position "was being adopted after consultation with the accused."[6]

In practice, this meant that the testimony of the next witness, Mary Violet Power, also went before the jury without any examination or question. The account of Mary Power's extensive torture was just as powerful now as it had been the previous year. But significantly, she observed that Inouye merely felt for her pulse during her water torture, and he was not present when she was beaten by the interrogators. It was not until later that he suspended her upside down from a beam and proceeded to beat and kick her, as well as torture her with lighted cigarettes. The following day, the headline in the *South China Morning Post* read, "Hung Up and Burned ... Woman's Face Burned."[7]

The outrage of Kempeitai officers was sometimes focused on what seemed to be the most innocent activities. Dr. Vincente Atienza possessed a radio receiver that could receive foreign news, and upon learning of the Allied landings in France on June 6, 1944, he held an impromptu party to celebrate. Wong Pui, one of the locals, joined in. The police learned of the celebration, and on June 20, Atienza was arrested, hung from a beam for hours, and interrogated by Inouye. Atienza said that "on the whole accused [Inouye] took the initiative and asked the questions himself." He also saw Inouye questioning Wong Pui and later was assigned to give him medical aid, but "his back was burnt" and "practically no hope of survival."[8] There was a clear inference that while the prosecution could not prove that Inouye had murdered Wong Pui, he was one of the last of the torturers seen with him while he was still alive. Wong Pui's wife, Kwong Kam Sui, then testified. She remembered Inouye putting a question to her through George Wong: "Since you have so many children to look after why has your husband chosen to become a spy?"[9] She never saw her husband again and was later told that he died in prison. At the identification parade in Stanley Prison the previous February, Mrs. Kwong was among many Hong Kong residents who identified Inouye. However, unlike the others who were asked to tap him if they were able to make an identification, she refused to even touch him.

The Kempeitai suppression in 1944 seems to have been triggered by the news of the D-Day landings and renewed optimism in the civilian population that an end to the occupation was in sight. The previous year's crackdown was more severe, and many of the British Army Aid Group's operatives were seized and executed. David Loie, the head of the espionage unit in Kowloon and Victoria, was arrested. Rather than betray his comrades, he leaped to his death at the very Supreme Court building where Inouye's trial was in progress. On October 29, 1943, seven British internees and twenty-six Asians were beheaded at a mass execution. Actions against supposed spies increased in tempo after the D-Day news, "and in December [1944] the repression was still in full swing."[10] After years of being subjected to horrific treatment, most of it falling on the Chinese population, a jury now had one of the Kempeitai at its mercy. Moreover, he was not begging for mercy but, rather, had the audacity to take the position that he was justified in, and even proud of, what he had done.

While much of the testimony was a repeat of the previous trial, one witness who was referred to in an affidavit at previous proceedings now appeared in the flesh. Mohamed Yousif Khan,[11] one of a trio of Indian agents, confirmed that he was one of the "Three Musketeers," as John Power called them, who carried information to Allied spies and spread pro-British propaganda to Indian POWs. Prior to the war, Khan was an innocuous post office clerk. In August 1942, he was contacted by Major Clague of the BAAG and asked to meet with John Power and join his espionage ring. Khan brought along his brother Mohammed Hassan (Assan Khan) and a colleague, Ahmed Khan. The group was arrested on June 5, 1944, and confined in the Supreme Court building. Even under torture, all three denied their involvement with the British spy ring. On several occasions, Inouye suspended Yousif Khan from a beam and beat him at length, ordering him to confess to being a spy. Three times Khan was given the water torture and each time Inouye took part. Finally, in a bizarre twist, Inouye took all three of the Indian agents to a workshop and ordered them to kneel facing Tokyo. They were no longer required, he told them, and they were about to die. But if they would supply information on the spy operations of the BAAG, they might yet be set free. The Khans, however, denied having any knowledge. In that case, Inouye inquired whether they wanted their bodies to be buried or burned. When they refused to react, he became furious and began to strike them, calling out that as they were Indians there was no excuse for their conduct and that they would be shot. However, they were released on parole. Obviously the decision was previously made to release Khan and the others due to lack of proof. Inouye had mounted this last-minute charade to try and induce a confession.

Those witnesses who were not spies included several Hong Kong women whose husbands or sons were arrested by a party of police that may have included Inouye. Mrs. Maria Lee, who gave her testimony in Spanish, recounted that her son Enrique never returned from prison, but there was no suggestion that Inouye was in any way responsible. Chan Wai Mui, the wife of suspected spy Henry Chang, knew Inouye well as he came many times to their house to look for radios and to interrogate her. Once her husband was arrested and tortured to death, she was taken in and was "beaten by both accused [Inouye] and Moriyama with a long whip." The men used one whip and exchanged it in turn when one grew tired of beating her.[12] Felizerto Sequeira, another British spy, was tortured by having pieces of cotton wool dipped in alcohol, ignited, and deposited on his head or inside his shirt by Inouye. The previous February, during an identification parade, Sequeira had been confronted with a lineup that included Inouye. He immediately identified him and called out, "The accused must die this time and that he was a bastard."[13] This stultifying procession of witnesses went on and on, for prosecutor Lonsdale had apparently concluded that quantity was the best way to secure a conviction. Undoubtedly the barrage of horror stories where Inouye was an active participant in torture must have resonated with the jury.

All of these prolonged torture sessions were largely futile for the Kempeitai, and the near drowning or whipping of suspects failed to elicit any helpful information. Albert Guest, the government wireless operator, received several rounds of the water torture from Inouye. He was tied up on a bathroom floor, a towel placed over his face, and water pumped into him.

Inouye occasionally jumped on his stomach to force water back up into his system. All the while, Inouye promised Guest that it would stop if he would simply admit to being a spy. Guest was in reality an active spy and had been operating a wireless communication network with the Allies and supplying "information about local movements of troops shipping and abt. the results of Allied bombing."[14] But Guest did not break, and his true identity and activities were never found out.

The police counterespionage efforts seemed entirely hit or miss. As one observer noted, "The unfortunates subjected to torture generally admitted anything the Japanese wanted them to say, no matter where the truth lay, or died resisting. Thus, alongside accurate information, intelligence gleaned through torture was often misinformation confirmed."[15] Frequently, the purpose of torture was merely to save face. Even when the wrong person was arrested, they were still tortured on the basis that they might be guilty of something. Dev Saran Das, a civil servant, was interrogated by Inouye, tortured by the Kempeitai, and sentenced to five years imprisonment for spreading news from Allied radios. He had no connections to the BAAG and had never worked against the Japanese. Wong Chung never spied for the British but was nevertheless beaten and tortured by Inouye and confessed in order to make it stop: "I confessed though I had done nothing and was sentenced to 12 yrs. imprison."[16] Despite the brutality of their methods, the Kempeitai was ineffective in obtaining useful information and ferreting out the spy networks that infiltrated the city.

What was the point to all of these witnesses? If the accusation against Inouye was that he was a traitor, then simply assisting the Japanese police as an interpreter in two cases was sufficient to prove the charge. The issue was loyalty, not mistreatment. However, the array of witnesses — twenty-seven in all — recounting incidents of his callous actions was intended to inflame the jurors' sentiments against him. All of this was exceptionally emotional evidence, and Inouye's counsel did nothing to try and stop it. Interestingly, the prosecution also called witnesses who confirmed that Inouye had done little or nothing to them. Ame Madar confirmed that the "accused was only interpreting."[17] William Low, a law clerk, swore that the "accused did not question me or touch me." Lai Chak Po stated that he was interrogated but not tortured by Moriyama, with Inouye simply handling the translations. If Loseby had made attempts to highlight their testimony by cross-examining them and raising doubt that Inouye was as consistently evil as the prosecution alleged, he might have diminished the impact of the torture stories. However, he did nothing.

It all led to the fourth and final day of trial, when the only defence witness, Kanao Inouye himself, would take the stand. The *China Mail* reported that on the morning of Thursday, April 18, many European spectators were present. Far more than a cheap spectacle, this trial was about to enable them to see the enemy in the flesh. They were not disappointed.

11

EXHIBIT C

DESPITE WHAT THEY HAD ALREADY READ OR HEARD, THE JURORS WERE about to hear a vastly different account of Inouye's early life. The previous version, given at his war crimes trial a year before, described his idyllic child-hood in Canada, his uneasiness in Japan, and his reluctant service as an interpreter with the military and the police. Many of the jurors likely read it in the newspapers or listened to it being discussed on the street. On April 18, the fourth day of trial, Inouye was about to spin a completely different story and wager his life that this latest version would be believed.

The Supreme Court was again packed with a capacity crowd of Europeans and Chinese to witness what had become a trial of the conduct of the Japanese occupation itself. Inouye began by explaining that it was true that he was born and raised in Canada, but both of his parents were Japanese. His name "Kanao" was given to him by his grandfather, and he stated that "I have regarded myself as Jap all the time."[1] In 1926, he travelled to Japan with his family. On the trip, his father died, leaving Kanao the *koshu*, or the head of the family. At the same time, he acquired a permanent registered address in Japan, at No. 7-3, Hongomotomachi, Hongo-ku, in Tokyo. He was too young to know under which passport he travelled to

Japan, but on the return trip to Canada, he was issued a Japanese passport. Thereafter, he received a yearly remittance of two thousand to four thousand yen from his grandfather. In September 1935, he again travelled to Japan with his mother but this time under the 1926 Japanese passport. Upon arrival, he registered with the district office at Hongo-ku. While his mother returned to Canada, he resolved to stay and make a new life for himself in Japan: "I left no home behind me in Canada in 1935.... I intended that my home was to be in Japan for the future."[2] He paid his respects to his father's grave and then enrolled at the Waseda Kokusai Gakuin, a prep school for university. He found himself perfectly comfortable in the land of his ancestors: "I was treated as if I had lived in Japan all my life. My friends in Japan had not different mentality to friends in Canada."[3] His studies were interrupted in 1936 when he was obliged to take the military examination required of all Japanese males before they turned twenty-one. As a result of this examination, he was conscripted into the army on March 1, 1937. He swore allegiance to the emperor and proudly added, "All Japanese subjects have the blood of the Emperor in their veins."[4]

Inouye then referred to a remarkable document introduced by the prosecution that had escaped notice so far. As Sub-Inspector Percy Lowe of the Hong Kong Police took him into custody on November 27, 1946, after he was transferred from military to civilian control, Lowe found a Japanese document on him. Inouye seemed agitated when the police officer took it and Inouye asked for permission to destroy it as it would be of no interest to the police. Lowe declined to do so and preserved the document, although he made no attempt to translate it at the time or determine its relevance. It was entered into evidence as Exhibit "C." Inouye explained that it was a record written by an interpreter named Tsuta at his direction since he could not properly write Japanese. The exhibit presented to the Court was a typed version in English that Inouye identified as correct except that he was not conscripted into the Kempeitai in 1944 as it recorded, but he had volunteered. Exhibit C laid out a radically different biography of the accused.

According to Exhibit C, Inouye was accepted as an A grade candidate for recruitment into the Imperial Japanese Army in June 1936. In March 1937, he began military service and was attached to the Manchurian Independent

EXHIBIT C

Defence Unit, the Third Company, Seventh Battalion, under Col. Takamori Takashi. This unit was tasked with defending the Manchurian rail connection to Japan. In February 1938, he was transferred to the First Company of the Fifth Border Battalion at Sho-Muton, Manchuria, under Lieutenant Colonel Nagasawa. At the same time, he was promoted to private first class, but after only a few weeks of service he was admitted to a military hospital for catarrh, or a buildup of mucous in his lungs. He was transferred to a Tokyo hospital, where his condition did not improve. Discharged from the army in January 1939, he was given a disabled soldier award. The remainder of the document detailed his attending an agricultural school from 1939 to 1940, a brief stint in a Tokyo sanatorium, as well as his service at a POW camp and as a Kempeitai interpreter. Lastly, it added that in April 1945, he was again conscripted into the army and served in the Hong Kong Defence Unit until the surrender in August 1945. Altogether, he received four military awards.

In the early stages of the war, the Imperial Army was reluctant to conscript Nisei with limited fluency in Japanese and whose loyalty was suspect. Author Carey McWilliams noted that "the Nisei have always been misfits in Japan" and many had difficulty with the language. This reluctance diminished as the war progressed, and many of the twenty thousand Nisei who lived in Japan at the war's outbreak either volunteered or were conscripted into service. For many of them, their fluency in English would be valuable and they were used to monitor Allied communications or to deal with prisoners.[5]

Inouye's record of service coincided with Japan going to war with Nationalist China after the Marco Polo Bridge incident, in July 1937. Since Japan conquered northeastern China, or Manchuria, and set up the puppet state of Manchukuo in 1931, the two countries were in a state of semiconflict. By the summer of 1937, all-out war broke out, and fighting raged through northern China and a major battle developed around Shanghai. According to Inouye's account, he avoided all this and instead served in Manchuria, where there was little fighting.

In any event, the account of Inouye's service as recorded in Exhibit C was clear and consistent. It provided in minute detail the units he served in, as well as his commanding officers. Moreover, he was clearly proud of his military record and his work with the Kempeitai, catching spies: "I knew we were to do everything for counter espionage work but not treacherously." When Chief Justice Blackall asked him what he meant by "treacherously," Inouye replied, "I mean we were to arrest there [sic] persons but not kill them right off or things like that."[6] He added that there was no shame in working for the emperor: "The English King was our enemy at the time. Did not think I owed him any allegiance by reason of my birth. To my knowledge I did not owe him any."[7]

The purpose of Exhibit C was never explained, and no one asked Inouye why he went to the trouble to hire a scribe to detail his previous military record. It is possible that he wanted to leave an account so that his wife and child might be able to make a claim for benefits after his death, or to preserve his family's honour. If so, then why did he try to destroy Exhibit C in November 1946? He was neither asked, nor did he offer an explanation. Perhaps he needed to get rid of any background material that conflicted with his intention to fabricate a story whereby he never served in the military or felt at home in Japan. If he portrayed himself to his captors as a reluctant enemy, they might see him as one of their own and be hesitant to punish him. At least that was the initial version of his past life provided to the war crimes trial. He now explained that he willingly served in Japan's military, and by so doing, felt that he was serving his true homeland.[8] Canada was never his country; it was a land of grinding prejudice and discrimination to the extent that he became embittered against all Canadians. When asked to elaborate, he pointed out that he could not vote, go to a medical or law school, or get a government job — all of which was true.[9] If he remained in the country of his birth after the start of the war, he would most likely have been uprooted and compelled to work on road construction or in the sugar beet fields. Canada never accepted him as one of its own, so what obligation did he bear toward it?

Cross-examined by Lonsdale, Inouye stuck rigorously to his new story. He recounted how surprised defence counsel Haggan was when he spoke clear English. After he explained that he was born in Canada, Haggan said that there must be some mistake and he should be tried for treason

EXHIBIT C

rather than war crimes. Inouye then explained that he was registered in Japan as a subject and that all Japanese who were in the country in 1942 were registered as subjects. After he was sentenced to death at his first trial, Inouye hoped that the part of the petition in which he claimed Canadian nationality would save his life. But in any case, the petition was written by Haggan and it was his idea that Inouye should claim to be a Canadian citizen. Citizenship was obviously the key issue, and Lonsdale pursued the point. The *South China Morning Post* recorded the following interchange:

> LONSDALE: After you became 21 years of age, did you put your hand to any document formally making yourself a naturalized Japanese subject?
> INOUYE: Yes.
> LONSDALE: Have you put your hand to a document formally?
> INOUYE: Yes.
> LONSDALE: What document?
> INOUYE: I have my koseki toho [a koseki tohon is a copy of the family register or domicile].
> CHIEF JUSTICE: Did you regard your registration in Japan as naturalization?
> INOUYE: Yes, as a Japanese subject because it was through that that I was conscripted. I owe my allegiance to the Japanese Emperor.[10]

It was clear that Inouye had never taken any real steps to become naturalized because he felt it was unnecessary since he already considered himself fully Japanese: "I never registered myself as a Canadian national. I always considered myself as a Japanese national."[11] Lonsdale asked if there was a document that proved this. Inouye replied, "I put my chop [personal seal] to the military conscription paper," an act that only a true Japanese citizen could do.

At this juncture, Chief Justice Blackall stopped the proceedings and asked Inouye a specific question. In the British legal system, the trial judge usually remains aloof and lets the lawyers guide the flow of evidence; it was rare for a judge to interject himself into the examinations. The importance of Blackall inserting himself into the process might not have been apparent at the time, but it would have a significant impact on the outcome of the case. He asked if Inouye had ever inquired into ways of renouncing his Canadian nationality. Inouye replied that there was no reason to do so "because I always as [*sic*] a Jap. subject."[12] In Inouye's view, he was thoroughly Japanese, and the last contact he had with his Canadian family was mailing his mother a remittance of one thousand yen in the summer of 1941. The chief justice did not pursue the matter further.

Lonsdale resumed the cross-examination and inquired if it was true that Inouye had once been arrested by the Kempeitai and given the water torture. Inouye was reluctant to answer and insisted it was a personal affair. Blackall ordered him to respond. Inouye then confirmed his previous account, that in 1935 or 1936 he was indeed given the water torture by the Kempeitai "because I had Nisei friends,"[13] also adding that this in no way swayed him from his devotion to the emperor.

Lonsdale went on to remind him that his answers were given at the war crimes trial under a Christian oath. Inouye said that he was not a Christian and could not remember his previous answers. When challenged with his previous testimony of less than a year earlier — that he was happy in Canada and felt out of place in Japan — he responded with a litany of "can't remembers." It was apparent that Inouye's current testimony contradicted almost everything he had previously sworn to. Before, he said that he joined the Kempeitai in a last-ditch effort to stay in Hong Kong with his wife. Inouye now replied that he could not recollect that answer and that he came to Hong Kong to work in a civilian firm and to serve the emperor. Well, which one was it? Instead of writhing under cross-examination, Inouye decided to divert attention from the inconsistencies and sprang to attention in the witness box and shouted in Japanese: "My body is the Japanese Emperor's body — my mind and body belong to the Japanese Emperor and he can do what he likes with it."[14]

A few moments later, he again came to attention, clicked his heels, and called out in Japanese, "Long live the Emperor!" The chief justice peered down at the witness and sighed. "There was no need to be theatrical."[15]

EXHIBIT C

On the contrary, there was every need to be theatrical. Inouye was playing to an audience of jurors who had already been coached on his first story that portrayed him as a reluctant warrior but an opportunistic torturer. Now he had to make them believe that he was Japanese through and through. A devoted soldier of his emperor, he had done distasteful but necessary things on behalf of his country. One can imagine Inouye, standing erect before the court, adopting a proud military bearing that was so much in contrast to his previous demeanour as the inoffensive translator. It would take some playacting and probably some exaggeration to convince a jury of this new narrative.

Inouye insisted that he did not consider himself to be a Canadian and he had no intention of ever returning to Canada. "You will never be given another opportunity,"[16] Lonsdale observed. Perhaps in an attempt to mitigate his conduct, Inouye added that he did not appreciate the brutal methods used by the Kempeitai, and "he acted only as an interpreter and unless ordered to take part in the beatings, took no action of his own."[17] When confronted with the mass of evidence against him, Inouye denied that he tortured anyone and that in several cases, he did not even know the victims. During the cross-examination, the prosecution brought out a great deal of information that was overlooked by the accused's lawyer. Inouye was given the opportunity to review the evidence of each witness against him before giving his version of events. To cite one example, Inouye swore that Albert Guest, the government wireless operator, was a prisoner of a Sergeant Kaki, not Moriyama, and therefore Inouye was not even called on to interpret. Inouye gave a blanket denial of Guest's accusations: "Everything he said about me is untrue."[18] Chief Justice Blackall asked him if it was true that he made suspects kneel in the direction of Tokyo before their execution. Inouye denied that as well, for "it would have been a disgrace to the Japanese to make them do so."[19] Apparently, all the prosecution witnesses were liars and the only honest man in the courtroom was Kanao Inouye. However, having waived his right to cross-examine the victims, their testimony of his conduct remained damning and undiminished.

In response to a question from Lonsdale, Inouye confirmed that he once had several documents attesting to his Japanese nationality, including the registration papers from the Waseda prep school and an identification card that he was a Tokyo resident. All of these were lost at the time of his arrest. To compound his beleaguered defence he had asked that replacement documents be forwarded from Japan but none had arrived. Once the cross-examination concluded, the chief justice asked Loseby if he needed time to find any additional documents. Inexplicably, Loseby replied that it would not be necessary. His commitment to his client's defence seemed perfunctory at best. This completed the evidence, and the lawyers turned to the jury to plead their cases.

Crown prosecutor Lonsdale suspected that Inouye would claim that he had dual nationality, but the only way to prove dual nationality would be to place an expert in Japanese law on the stand, which never happened. Clearly, Inouye was bound by allegiance to the British Crown due to his Canadian birth. It was irrelevant that he committed his traitorous acts in Hong Kong, since his allegiance bound him wherever he was in the world to support the king against his enemies. But was it really that simple? Less than a year before Inouye's trial, Charles Cousens, an Australian officer who was coerced into helping the Japanese make propaganda broadcasts, was charged under the same treason statute. Although he was committed for trial, the charges were soon dropped since it was apparent that all his actions were under threat of torture.

A more famous and compelling case arose from the "Tokyo Rose" trial. Tokyo Rose was a series of female radio performers who sent out demoralizing messages to Allied, mostly American, soldiers. One performer in particular, Iva D'Aquino, was arrested by the Americans shortly after the end of the war. Born in Los Angeles, she was visiting an ill relative in Japan when the war began, and she became trapped in the country. Despite pressure from the Japanese government, she refused to renounce her allegiance to the United States. As an alien resident, she was scraping by until she was recruited by Radio Tokyo to make propaganda statements and play music directed to Allies. Arrested after the war, she was released after a year when it was determined that most Allied troops considered her broadcasts light entertainment. Working with Charles Cousens, her program provided information to the Allies on the condition of the POWs. However, U.S. zealots

EXHIBIT C

sought out this "Mata Hari of radio" and she was charged with treason in 1948. In 1949, she was convicted on one count and sentenced to ten years.[20] Both the Cousens and D'Aquino cases highlighted that treason was not necessarily as straightforward as the Crown prosecutor made it out. Cousens had little choice but to act as he did; likewise, D'Aquino did what she could to carry on as an alien in Japan. Both were doing what they thought they had to do to survive. Was it the same with Inouye?

For the defence, Loseby rose and pointed out to the jurors that his client was not on trial for torture. He had indeed acted to stop espionage against the Japanese administration of Hong Kong, but if he was a Japanese citizen, he was entitled, and perhaps even required, to do so. Burrowing down to the core of the case, Loseby proposed that the question the jury had to decide was where Inouye's loyalties lay. It was a question that the prosecution had all but avoided and they were negligent in failing to bring up evidence on this key point. The Crown prosecution had Exhibit C in their possession since November 1946, but had done nothing to confirm or deny its validity. It was this exhibit that broke the case wide open and should have been followed up by the police. It proved that Inouye consistently considered himself a Japanese citizen to the extent that he had given his oath to the emperor and served him in war. It was true that Inouye was Canadian-born, but he was registered with the Japanese government as a subject since 1918, and at the very least, "he might have a dual nationality."[21]

If not brilliant, it was a serviceable summation. Loseby stressed the evidence that Inouye had a reasonable expectation that he was a Japanese citizen and acted accordingly. On that basis, there were no grounds to hold him liable for high treason to the British sovereign. While he did not stray into more philosophical areas, Loseby might have raised the question of "social membership." That is, to betray a group, one must belong to a group. As Inouye had testified, which was not rebutted, he was a second-class citizen in Canada. His ethnic origins prevented him from taking part in political life or advancing in a profession. How could he be disloyal to a group that rejected him in the first place?[22] On the other hand, the members of the jury might not have been susceptible to philosophical discussions of the nature of loyalty. It is far more likely that they were impressed by the stream of witnesses who testified to "Slap Happy's" humiliation and abuse of their friends and neighbours. The court then adjourned for the day, and the chief justice would sum up the case for the jury the following Tuesday.

•

The *China Mail* reported on the tension in the courtroom that morning and the "large crowd of European spectators present" with "seating accommodation ... fully occupied."[23] Sir Henry Blackall began his summation by telling the jury that he would try and explain some legal points as simply as he could. The facts were theirs to decide, but he was there to assist with legal interpretations. He appreciated that some of the jurors did not speak English as their first language so he would be as precise as possible. First, Inouye's case was widely publicized and it was likely that the jurors had already formed an opinion about him. Blackall asked them to do the impossible and "forget all about that"[24] in order to decide the case on the evidence. Still, the jurors were reminded not to forget that treason was a very serious matter:

> It is doubly so when it takes place in time of war and at a time when the British Empire was struggling against the powers of darkness. But at the same time, it is a principle of British Justice that no man, whatever he may be, can be convicted of a crime unless the evidence satisfies the jury beyond all reasonable doubt and in order to ensure perfect fairness, the Crown even in a case like this, brings in a counsel for the defence for the prisoner, and I may say so that the prisoner is fortunate is [*sic*] having been so ably defended by counsel for the defence.[25]

There was a good measure of self-congratulation to this declaration of a perfect administration of justice being administered to an individual who was admittedly a servant of the "powers of darkness." Blackall even praised the defence lawyer: "In some respect, Mr. Loseby's task may have

EXHIBIT C

been invidious, but it is the duty of members of the Bar to do everything they can for their clients."[26] There seemed to be a presumption in the judge's summation that while Inouye was doubtlessly guilty, the jurors should consider the lengths that the authorities went to provide him with a defence. The British sense of fair play had prevailed yet again, even in the instance of this apparently most unworthy recipient.

Chief Justice Blackall confirmed that Inouye was not on trial for torture, and the only issue was whether he breached the loyalty he owed to the British Crown. That did not stop Blackall from recounting in vivid detail the evidence of torture given by many of the witnesses. To decide the case, the jury had to understand the basics of British citizenship law. The birth certificate from British Columbia was cast-iron proof that Inouye was a natural-born British subject. There were only two ways to determine whether he divested himself of that citizenship. Where a person was a British subject through and through, he could take out naturalization in another state. The one caveat was that he could not change his nationality to that of a state with which his country was at war. However, if a person had a "dual nationality," and owed allegiance to another country due to his ethnic origins, he might make what is known as a declaration of alienage and cease to be a British subject. This legal document would have to be drawn up in conformity with the law to formally renounce British citizenship and be filed with the proper consular office in Tokyo. If Inouye had done so, he would not be liable for treason. A declaration of alienage could only have been made pursuant to section 14 of the British Nationality and Status of Aliens Act, 1914, or its equivalent in Canada, the Canadian Nationalization Act, 1914. But how likely was it that a nineteen-year-old with a limited high school education arriving in Japan in 1935 was aware of these obscure statutes? For that matter, he could not even invoke these laws until he turned twenty-one in 1937, by which time he had already sworn his oath to the emperor and was serving him in Manchuria. How fair was it to conclude that whether he lived or died should be determined on filing the proper paperwork according to a law he had never heard of?

To Chief Justice Blackall, it was terribly relevant. Now he explained the importance of the question he asked Inouye the previous day. During that exchange, he specifically asked Inouye whether he had ever filed a declaration of alienage denying his British citizenship. When Inouye confirmed that he had not, it was therefore settled that Inouye remained a British subject. Inouye maintained that by joining the Imperial Japanese Army in 1937 and swearing loyalty to the emperor, he manifested his loyalty to Japan. Blackall leaned down and told the jurors that Inouye was confused since merely joining a foreign army did not expunge British nationality. Blackall all but dismissed the notion of dual nationality that Loseby had suggested. It was either one or the other. Failure to formally renounce his British citizenship meant that he remained British. Whatever validity this had in the fine points of English law, it seemed a stretch that anyone in Inouye's position had any notion of what a declaration of alienage was.

Blackall continued that Inouye thought it a fine thing to volunteer for the Kempeitai and that by doing so, he was serving his real country. Inouye's ample testimony that he felt ill-used in Canada and that he had a grievance against the Anglo-Saxon race introduced the critical issue of his motivations. Blackall illustrated the point by referring to the case of the German consul Ahlers at the beginning of the First World War. Ahlers assisted German nationals in returning home while Britain was neutral but continued in this task even after the declaration of war between Britain and Germany on August 4, 1914. After his conviction for high treason, the British Appeal Court ruled that it should have been left with the jury to determine if he was "acting evilly" or if he was merely doing what he was entitled and bound to do. Lord Reading ruled that "a Man is not guilty of treason unless he intends to betray England."[27] The chief justice left a similar question with the jury:

> So gentlemen, you will have to consider was his intention an evil one and was his intention to assist the King's enemies, or did he believe that he was not only entitled, but bound to act in the way he has done....
>
> Now, gentlemen, that is the question for you. If you consider that he was purely actuated by the belief that he was carrying out his duty honestly, then you should give him the benefit of that. If, on the other hand, you consider

EXHIBIT C

he was intending and mainly concerned in assisting the
King's enemies, well then, you ought to find him guilty.[28]

This placed the jurors in a most unusual position. They were being
instructed that it was up to them to look into Inouye's mind and determine
what motivated him. Facts can be apparent, and it was a fact that he had
been born in Kamloops, British Columbia. That he served the Kempeitai
and bound up prisoners and assisted with the water torture were also facts.
But whether he did these acts out of a patriotic motive to serve his country,
or whether he did so for "evil motives," was difficult to answer. The trial
judge had left the jurors with the challenging task of trying to determine a
person's deepest impulses.

This task was all the more difficult because Blackall previously
instructed the jury that the case was to be decided solely on the basis of
Inouye's citizenship. Since Inouye failed to file the declaration of alienage,
he therefore remained British. If he was British, his acts were high treason;
if he was Japanese, his acts might constitute war crimes. But in light of the
reasoning in the *Ahlers* case, if the jury concluded that Inouye *thought* that
he was Japanese, did that absolve his service in the Kempeitai? By now,
even those jurors who were proficient in English must have been baffled
as to the standard they were expected to apply. This confusion became apparent a few moments before the jury left the courtroom to consider their
verdict. The foreman rose and asked the judge a question that likely had
been bothering several of them. "Do you direct," he asked Blackall, "that
he [Inouye] was definitely never a Japanese subject?"[29] This was a question of fact for the jury to determine. With Inouye's record of swearing
allegiance to the Japanese emperor and serving in Manchuria, there was
now ample evidence before them that he acted as, and felt himself to be,
a Japanese subject. The jurors also had the registration certificate of 1918
as well as his travelling on a Japanese passport in 1935. In order to resolve
the question of citizenship, the jurors could accept or reject this evidence,
and it was not a decision the judge was entitled to make or to override.
Nevertheless, Blackall looked down on the jurors and replied with a simple
"yes." In so doing, the chief justice effectively put Kanao Inouye's head in

the noose. If he was not Japanese, then he was British and a traitor. Loseby sat by and made no objection.

The jury retired. Within ten minutes, they were back in the courtroom. Throughout the summation, Inouye had sat in the prisoner's dock and listened with rapt fascination to Blackall's direction. As Inouye stood and faced the jury, he "shuddered slightly and stiffened as he heard the foreman of the jury announce the verdict"[30] that they unanimously found him guilty of high treason. The chief justice donned the black cap, the symbol that a judge was about to order the taking of a life, and for the second time, Kanao Inouye heard the sentence of death pronounced against him.

12

TECHNICALITIES OF LAW

AFTER THE PASSING OF SENTENCE ON APRIL 22, 1947, INOUYE WOULD be known to the Hong Kong prison system solely by his classification, "Condemned Prisoner No. 528 INOUYE KANAO."

While Loseby's interest in the case waned as soon as the legal aid payments stopped, solicitor Woo made himself available to assist Inouye with filing an appeal. The appeal consisted of a petition[1] handwritten by Inouye two days after his sentence of death to the governor of Hong Kong. In his fine, clear penmanship, he listed the reasons why he was a Japanese subject. From the registration of his birth with the Japanese Consul in February 1919, to the assumption of his father's role as head of the family at its Tokyo address in 1926, to his enlistment in the army in 1936 and war service since 1937, Inouye had lived his life as a Japanese citizen. The documents that verified all this should have been presented at his trial — had his lawyer considered asking for an adjournment — and they were still not available to him. In any case, he had "only acted in the capacity of a simple interpreter"[2] under the orders of senior police officers.

Two weeks after the end of the trial, the documents proving Inouye's residency in Tokyo arrived in Hong Kong. The identity paper of permanent domicile showed that Kanao Inouye was a resident of the Hongo-ku district of Tokyo. The document's original was incinerated in the Tokyo firestorm of March 10, 1945, but other surviving records confirmed that according to the census register, he was a citizen of that community and the head of his family since the death of his father in 1926. A further government document verified his conscription in 1936, service in Manchuria in 1937, and discharge for medical reasons in January 1939.[3] If available for the court, these documents would have been powerful evidence that contrary to Blackwell's conclusion, Inouye was actually a Japanese citizen.

A month after his petition was filed, Inouye was back in a courtroom to find out if a panel of appeal judges would hear him. A reporter for the *China Mail* was present and thought that his appearance had changed: "Inouye has lost much weight since his last appearance in Court. The air of confidence which he displayed during the original trial has disappeared, and Inouye sat hunched in the dock, closely following every word uttered by his counsel."[4] Appearing with him was Loseby, who was again appointed defence counsel. Whether Inouye wanted him or not was irrelevant as it appeared that he was the only lawyer the government was willing to provide. Loseby began by noting for the Court that he was hired for the purposes of the appeal for a week and did not have adequate time to prepare. The essence of the appeal was nationality: "Inouye denied that he was, at any material time, a British subject. It was the contention of Inouye that he assisted at all material times as a Japanese subject."[5] While many witnesses testified that "Inouye acted vigorously and even cruelly," the only question that should have been decided was his allegiance. In an interesting aside, Loseby promised that his upcoming appeal would deal with the case of the infamous "Lord Haw-Haw" William Joyce. That case had already caused rumblings within the British legal establishment, and to many, the verdict and execution were a travesty and more about revenge than justice. Loseby suggested that similar arguments could be made on Inouye's behalf, which might prevent another miscarriage of justice. The judges deferred comments on the subject, but Justice Williams agreed that the application was important and granted Loseby further time to prepare.

By the summer of 1947, the war was beginning to fade from memory in Hong Kong and more pressing concerns were coming to the forefront. While the colony's population declined to half a million during the Japanese occupation, many residents returned, along with refugees from the interior. The city's housing stock was badly depleted during the war years and one politician denounced the situation: with residents "packed in their hot, insanitary, un-private quarters, they must be sick of promises and of words."[6] Popular unrest led to a bus strike in June and a massive strike by dockyard workers protesting low wages in August. In other ways, Hong Kong was slowly returning to its prewar normalcy. In June, the Kennedy Town Dragon Boat Race attracted over two thousand spectators from all classes. Preparations were also underway for the second anniversary of the British re-entry into the colony. The Hong Kong Cricket Club would be the site for the celebrations featuring various British regiments on parade. On this occasion the public could attend on the parade ground, although the clubhouse remained reserved for members only. The return of the racial hierarchy was beginning to irk, and one RAF veteran with a Eurasian background was disgusted by the general attitude of "snobbery, the smugness, the lack of tolerance"[7] displayed by the colony's elite. During the conflict, he was welcomed into society, but now the "pukka" clubs would not admit him. During Inouye's trial, it was apparent how many of the ordinary people of Hong Kong risked their lives to assist British intelligence and several had paid a high price for their service, but none of them would be welcomed as members of the Cricket Club.

On July 1, 1947 — Dominion Day back in the country of Kanao Inouye's birth — the Full Court assembled to hear the appeal. Ironically, it was the same day that military and civil officials honoured the 228 Canadian dead who were being reburied in the Sai Wan War Cemetery. Two thousand British Commonwealth and Empire servicemen were eventually interred in Sai Wan along with a memorial to those whose remains were never found. These sacrifices were not far from mind.

Loseby's appeal argument over the next two and a half hours stuck to the original position that Inouye had always been a Japanese subject, therefore he could not be guilty of high treason. Since the recently arrived information from Japan proving Inouye's Japanese citizenship was not available for the trial, it could not be used on the appeal. Loseby's sheer incompetence in failing to seek an adjournment so that this information could be provided was now likely to prove fatal to his client. This left Loseby with only a legal argument to use on the appeal, and his most telling point was Blackall's direction to the jury that Inouye was not a Japanese citizen. While the judge told the jurors at the beginning of his summation that they were to be the deciders of fact, this was never intended to be a hollow admonition. It had to be followed by a sincere deference by the judge to the jurors on factual matters. Instead, the trial judge ordered the jury to conclude that Inouye was not a Japanese citizen. On the fundamental issue of loyalty and citizenship, the judge had erroneously withdrawn the issue from the jury. This was clearly wrong, and Loseby suggested that the jurors should have been told that based on the evidence before them, "it is for you to make up your own mind what to believe and what is not to believe on the subject."[8]

Loseby referred to the dissenting opinion of Privy Councillor Lord Porter in the infamous "Lord Haw-Haw" case of William Joyce. Porter also thought that nationality was a question that could only be decided by the jury, and whether or not Joyce's passport renewal extended his duty of allegiance was an issue solely in their discretion. In Joyce's case, his reliance on a British passport was the only reason the trial judge concluded that he was a British subject, and in so doing, he had taken the citizenship question out of the jury's hands. Loseby argued that the same mistake was made in this case by the judge's direction to the jury that Inouye was never a Japanese citizen.[9] Moreover, the evidence in Inouye's case was that he travelled in 1935 under a Japanese passport and had never requested a British passport since he was not British. This vital piece of evidence might have persuaded the jury that unlike Joyce, Inouye was not a British subject and could not have committed treason. Loseby conceded that Joyce was an "odious person"[10] and a shameless Nazi and implied that his client's character was also far from sterling; nevertheless, personal conduct was not an issue to be considered on the assessment of loyalty. The judgment should not have been "clouded on that account."[11]

The prosecution countered that Blackall's summation was eminently fair. The facts were that Inouye was born in Canada and he was a subject of the king. Inouye also acknowledged to the judge that he had not taken any steps to renounce his Canadian citizenship. Having failed to file the proper paperwork, the jury was all but obliged to concur that he retained British allegiance. Crown prosecutor Lonsdale simply refused to deal with the *Ahlers* precedent and the right of the jury to consider the totality of Inouye's actions to determine if he truly felt that he was a Japanese citizen.

When the court reconvened on July 16, it seemed that the two judges who made up the appeal panel, Williams and Gould, were hesitant in making their ruling. After all, they were reviewing a decision of Chief Justice Blackall, the leading figure in the local judiciary. As a judge who had filled important posts across the British Empire, contradicting him could not be good for one's career. They retraced the summation and found no fault in it. They agreed that merely joining the Japanese army did not alter Inouye's citizenship and that nationality was not a matter of personal belief but a question of law. Nevertheless, they were uneasy about Blackall's direction to the jury that they had to assume that Inouye was not a Japanese citizen. Blackall had taken it upon himself to decide the key factual issue that was in the jury's discretion to decide. In so doing, Williams and Gould tepidly felt that "the Judge's direction is open to criticism here in that it might appear he was taking the decision on the facts out of their hands."[12] Even though Blackall may have been incorrect, the two judges reconciled themselves with the notion that the jury could override his comments, though it seemed unlikely that a group of men who were not highly educated with no experience in law would overrule a chief justice. Perhaps it was a miscue, but in their opinion, it was not one big enough to alter the result.

The judges then referred to the *Ahlers* case, in which the consul in Britain assisted German citizens to return home to fight against Britain. This was to be distinguished from Inouye's case, they concluded, in that Inouye admitted he was working to stop British espionage. Yet how this distinguished the two situations is impossible to tell. In both cases, persons who were nominally British but who held allegiances to other countries, served those countries in war. Ahlers was helping young Germans return to Germany to fight and kill Englishmen; Inouye was trying to stop espionage against Japanese forces. The principles in both situations were the same, and it was illogical to exonerate Ahlers while condemning Inouye. Nevertheless, the appeal judges concluded that in its totality, the summation was not only appropriate but also that it "remained on the whole rather in favour of the accused."[13]

For the third time, Kanao Inouye rose to his feet and listened to a court pronounce the sentence of death on him.

•

Less than a week later, Chief Justice Sir Henry Blackall reported to the governor on the outcome of the legal proceedings. While Blackall publicly emphasized that the charge against Inouye was high treason and not linked to atrocities, in reality the latter was uppermost in the judge's mind, and the admission of the many instances of torture was appropriate to establish Inouye's traitorous purpose. He listed the forms of torture in which Inouye took part: "Counsel for the defence did not cross-examine these witnesses, and although the prisoner denied some of these allegations when in the witness box, the evidence of his cruelties was overwhelming and showed him to be a callous and sadistic brute who well deserved his nickname of 'Slap Happy.'"[14] With this comment, Blackall let slip that it was the nature of Inouye's activity, and not the actual disloyalty, that mattered most. Blackall held that if Inouye had served simply as a soldier, as an "honourable combatant,"[15] that his sentence should be commuted. However, since Inouye voluntarily joined the Tokko section and committed war crimes while there, a military court thought he should suffer death.

There was also the question of whether Inouye held dual citizenship. Blackall also waved this aside and insisted that since Inouye was born in Canada, he was always a British subject. Whether he was also a Japanese was irrelevant because he failed to take the necessary steps to divest himself of his status as a British subject. For all his lip service to the technical definition of treason and its roots in betrayal, in the end, the chief justice's decision was based on a revulsion of the events that occurred at 69 Kimberley Road.

Inouye had to die, not for an act of betrayal, but for what he had done to Mary Power and the others.

The final recourse was a desperate appeal to the Privy Council in London. Inouye was again without a lawyer and unable to file the required appeal in the proper form. His first attempt at a higher appeal was returned to him with a request that he state the legal reasons for his application. Although the trials and appeals appeared to be all but over, the Hong Kong press kept the Inouye case in the public eye. His name came up in some of the ongoing war crimes trials, which increased his infamy. In July 1947, at the trial of several other Kempeitai staff, the arrest and interrogation of Aaron Landau, proprietor of the popular "Jimmy's Kitchen," was raised. During the interrogation, Inouye kicked and punched Landau, and when the prisoner asked for water, Inouye "dipped a broom in a bucket of human excreta and wiped it over his face."[16] There would be no surge of popular sympathy on Inouye's behalf.

Inouye contacted authorities in Japan to expedite the forwarding of additional military and citizenship documents. Frustratingly, these letters were not being processed since they did not pass the military censor. On July 22, the requests were rejected by Tokyo, and the letters were "condemned by SCAP Civil Censorship Division."[17] Since his case was now a civilian and not a military one, the Allied forces in Japan saw no need to expedite his request. At least the local prison officials were sympathetic. On July 28, the commissioner of prisons asked the Land Forces — ironically to the attention of Captain Haggan — the following: "Condemned Prisoner Inouye Kanao requests that his letters be sent by Air-mail. May this be done please?"[18]

Inouye then turned to the Japanese civil government for help. Writing to the minister of justice, Kimura Tokutaro, he requested his registration as a Japanese citizen, which was required before he took the physical examination to enter the army. He was sure that his Uncle Asada arranged for this beforehand. He also asked for his identification card and 1926 passport. Lastly, in what can only be seen as a delusional gesture, he asked the minister to forward five thousand dollars in U.S. funds for his defence. It did not seem to register with him that the Japanese government did not have such funds available, and in any event, it was far too late to change the course of his case. It was apparent to everyone except Inouye that the carousel of trials and appeals was at its end.

By the beginning of August, with little time remaining until the execution, which was scheduled for August 26, the Full Court again met to determine whether Inouye could seek leave to appeal to the Judicial Committee of the Privy Council, the highest appeal court in the British Empire. They admitted to some confusion and applied to the secretary of state for the colonies for direction. A memo followed in which the secretary cited a 1930 case, *Chung Chuck v. The King*, as authority that colonial courts had no authority to grant leave to appeal to the Privy Council concerning criminal matters. When the court went back into session on August 11, this case was brought up as deciding the issue. Loseby, who had returned as defence counsel, agreed and Inouye's last faint hope was extinguished.[19]

On August 15, with only eleven days remaining, Inouye filed a petition for mercy to the governor of Hong Kong, Sir Alexander Grantham. With some justification, he pointed out that the other Kempeitai staff, notably Moriyama, had disappeared and "the whole responsibilities have been thrown on my shoulders." He claimed that he was forced to serve in the Kempeitai for two years, and that he was only a *gunzoku*, a civilian staffer: "my duty was limited to interpreting and nothing else."[20] Even at this late stage, any attempt at honesty seemed beyond Inouye. But at last he was able to bring forward the original documents attesting to his Japanese civil status as well as his military record, which "arrived from Japan after my trial was concluded and hence I was not able to submit them to the Court."[21] It did not matter. The decision had been made and execution was only a matter of time. The governor's clerk already had prepared the necessary death warrant to empower the commissioner of prisons to execute Inouye on August 26. In a side note to the warrant, the clerk politely suggested to the governor that "the prisoner's petition of the 15th August should, of course, be seen by His Excellency before signature of the Warrant."[22]

Appearances were everything. With less than a week before the scheduled execution, Inouye wrote an appeal to King George VI. Refusing to accept his fate, Inouye's will to survive was persistent. Maintaining that he was a Japanese subject, Inouye repeated that he "served Japan to the best of his abilities as a true Japanese subject and at no time did your petitioner think that he was doing wrong."[23] He raised the same issues that were consistently rejected and added that he arrived at these unfortunate circumstances "in my ignorance of the technicalities of law of changing nationality."[24] It was all wasted effort. He would die for having failed to file the declaration of alienage to change his citizenship. A victim of paperwork, he would hang for neglecting to comply with the provisions of an obscure law he had never heard of. His last petition would not even leave Hong Kong prior to his execution. A tribute to bureaucracy, it was duly delivered in London a month later.

In the early morning of August 26, 1947, Kanao Inouye was bound up in ropes for execution. According to later accounts, he sang a patriotic song, "Umi Yukaba," as he was led from his cell and taken to the hanging chamber in Stanley Prison.[25] Just before the trap door opened, he shouted out a final salute to the emperor, "*Tenno Heika Banzai.*"

13

END OF A SCRUFFY SHOW

JUST WHO WAS KANAO INOUYE?

It seems impossible to capture a man who went to such great lengths to mask his heart's core. Was he the happy Canadian who was the "teacher's pet" in school and had gotten along with his white compatriots? Was he unable to culturally adapt to Japan, brutalized by the police, and forced to serve as a military interpreter? If this scenario is to be believed, then he remained more Canadian than Japanese. His wartime actions, including any beatings he administered, were all done under the force of orders he could not avoid. According to Arthur Rance, Inouye even entertained wistful notions of returning to Canada after the war. By portraying himself as a Canadian, Inouye might have hoped to avoid a severe penalty when he was judged by his own. This version also enabled the Canadian bureaucracy to avoid difficult questions as to his — and Japanese Canadians' — treatment in Canada.

Or was Inouye a devoted Japanese who in 1935 had returned to his homeland with no regrets about leaving the racist country that had repeatedly rejected and humiliated him? He had relocated to the land where he belonged, where he was like everyone else. Serving in his homeland's army was not a duty, but an honour. Fighting in Manchuria or interrogating spies in Hong Kong was all part of the fabric of being a patriotic Japanese during a time of war. Moreover, it also gave him the opportunity to express his fury against those Canadians who had once mistreated him. Viewed from these contrasting perspectives, loyalty was not always a straightforward proposition, and especially in a time of war, it might have different shades of meaning. This was especially true for a man such as Inouye, who lived on the margins in both of his worlds. The complexity of Inouye's identity as a Japanese Canadian and the duelling nature of his allegiances made his case unique, and one that the legal system of the day could not satisfactorily address.

Perhaps there may be some sympathy for Chief Justice Blackall, for in the context of the times, the concept of dual nationality was far from acceptable. In the early twentieth century, a citizen was expected to pledge his allegiance to one country. The Hague Convention of 1930 proclaimed as one of its ideals to seek the abolition of "all cases both of statelessness and of double nationality."[1] Only twenty states ratified the resulting convention. After the Second World War, with the expansion of diverse populations and the growth of minority communities around the world, many countries found ways to accommodate divided loyalties. By the late twentieth century, many states allowed for dual citizenship. This was acceptable as there was usually a low possibility for conflict between nations. But as the Inouye case demonstrated, such conflicts were possible, and the moral quandary of dual loyalty could have fatal consequences.

On the issue of citizenship, Inouye was apparently Canadian by birth and could claim Canadian citizenship; however, he also presented significant evidence that his allegiance lay exclusively with Japan. He had not only sworn loyalty to the emperor of Japan but had also served him in battle. No less a figure than Colonel Orr, the head of the war crimes detachment, concluded after reviewing Inouye's registration as a Japanese citizen and service in the Imperial Japanese Army, "If a man can abandon his previous allegiance by his own acts and declarations I should think that this man had gone about as far in indicating his intention as any reasonable law would require of him."[2] Orr was a perceptive observer, and it was apparent to him that determining the nature of Inouye's loyalties would not be a straightforward process. Unfortunately, the procedures applied to the case turned out to be disappointingly simplistic.

The question of dueling nationalities unsettled the Canadian government. Having dealt with the relocation of the Japanese Canadians during the war and offering their repatriation afterward, the last thing it needed was a showcase trial that had the potential to highlight the mistreatment of Canadian citizens because of their race. The horrors committed by Nazi Germany in the name of racial superiority shocked the world, and there was no need to bring up Canada's record of mistreatment of its racial minorities. Repatriating Inouye would have raised questions as to his supposed loyalty to a society that never accepted him in the first place. Moreover, despite Canada's sacrifices during the war, the Mackenzie King government had little interest in an expanded foreign policy or in the war crimes business. Canadian investigations in Europe were quickly wrapped up in early 1946, and there was only a limited contribution to the Asian war crimes process. It was so much cheaper to leave such matters to the great powers. After all, the British in Hong Kong were more than happy to raise their prestige by dealing with the individual who tortured so many of their colony's citizens. While so many of Inouye's colleagues had escaped, he was at hand and available to pay the price for what others had done.

Avoiding the political consequences of trying Inouye in Canada was one of the many political minefields the King government faced as a result of the Pacific war. Many in Canada wanted to know why an entire brigade had been placed in such a precarious position that it had been annihilated in a matter of days. A one-person royal commission to investigate sending "C" Force to Hong Kong was conducted by the country's leading judicial officer, Chief Justice Lyman Duff, in 1942. He concluded that there were persuasive political and military reasons to have dispatched "C" Force to Hong Kong.[3] It was a conclusion that would be challenged in later years, especially in Carl Vincent's *No Reason Why*.[4] It seemed that sending out two ill-trained battalions on what seemed to be a political gesture served no real military purpose. That it cost the lives of 557 Canadians seemed far too high a price to pay to bolster what everyone knew was already a hopeless defence. But it served the purpose of Prime Minister King to dampen any further discussion on Hong Kong, a topic that might be inflamed by the trial of a Japanese Canadian war criminal in Canada.

Kanao Inouye's execution that sultry August morning received only a perfunctory notice in Canada. The *Toronto Star* covered it in its back pages under the headline "Canadian-Born Jap Hanged in Hong Kong."[5] The report was barely longer than two paragraphs and contained few facts. His case raised so many difficult issues as to loyalty that his fellow Japanese Canadians were equally prepared to ignore it and move on. The report in the *New Canadian* was as brief and uninformative as that in the *Star.*[6] Almost two years after the execution, E.H. Norman of the Canadian Liaison Mission in Tokyo inquired as to what had happened to Kanao Inouye. His file, as well as that of the External Affairs Department, was still open and he wished to close the matter. Ottawa's officialdom was advised by the registrar of Canadian citizenship in June 1949 that Inouye was executed in 1947, and added with ironic understatement, "I would say, therefore, that this closes the file."[7]

Law schools attempt to instill in their pupils a reverence for the law as a rational, logical set of principles that brings order and stability to society. But in practice, the law is frequently an absurd exercise. One judicial academic concluded, "A trial, it is said, ought to be a search for the truth; instead it is often a game."[8] The case of Kanao Inouye is an example of the latter. When the issue was supposedly the nature of his loyalty, that question was put aside while the court fixated on his failure to comply with bureaucratic codes. There was no serious attempt to determine who Inouye was and where his loyalties truly lay. Perhaps it did not really matter as it was the nature of his actions that drove the judgment against him. The failure to file the required declaration of alienage became simply the pathway to conclude the game and get to the desired result.

The real difficulty in Inouye's case was the clash with allegiances and the issue of not one but a choice of national loyalties. His argument that he was at heart a citizen of Japan was plausible and deserved to be weighed on its merits. Unfortunately, it was not.

As for the sentence of death at the war crimes trial, defence lawyer Haggan tried to minimize Inouye's responsibility but conceded that he had

committed "petty tyrannies." Inouye had done far more than that, for he
had victimized and cruelly abused helpless individuals who had fallen under
his authority. While there was no proof that he killed anyone, he was responsible for immense pain and probably long-lasting psychological damage
inflicted on his many victims. For that, he unquestionably deserved severe
punishment. But as a minor war criminal, Inouye might be expected to
receive a prison sentence of five to ten years. Sentences are supposed to
be consistent and proportionate to the harm done. For example, a civilian
interpreter attached to the Kempeitai at Kuala Lumpur was found guilty
of a string of beatings and water tortures similar to those committed by
Inouye. He was sentenced to five years in prison.[9] Stodda, the chief interpreter at Sham Shui Po and an individual whose studied brutality mirrored
Inouye's, received only two years. A similar result was the norm for rank-
and-file interrogator-torturers. Colonel Stewart's comments that as Inouye
was properly educated and a Christian and should have known better took
his case out of the norm. Why that meant he was therefore more deserving
of a harsher sentence than that given to the ordinary Japanese prison guard
is hard to understand. Condemning Inouye to death for heavy-handed interrogations while giving far lighter sentences to other soldiers who were
responsible for multiple murders defied any logical explanation.

In Japan, the horrors of the war and the urgency of rebuilding made the
population try to put the issue of war crimes and war criminals behind them.
In December 1947, a magazine reported on the Tokyo trial of major war
criminals and noted how these men, so acclaimed in their day, were reviled
in defeat, with some facing execution and others "virtually forgotten."[10] A
lawyer, Yokota Kisaburo, who challenged Japan's policies back in the 1930s,
condemned the nationalist leaders. Under them, Japan "ignored treaties,
scorned justice and has committed horrendous atrocities."[11] There were rare
voices raised in shock when news of the horrors committed by the Japanese
army against innocent civilians and helpless prisoners became public. But
they were few, and as time wore on, the prisoners — especially the "minor"
war criminals — gained public sympathy in Japan. Over the years it seemed
to be the case that "the brutality and crimes committed by the Imperial
Japanese Army are dismissed or played down by nationalists who see the

focus of such events as evidence of a desire to blacken Japan's name."[12] By 1953, war criminals such as Niimori and Tokunaga, who committed crimes that made Inouye's pale by comparison, were repatriated. One returning ship was met by an enthusiastic crowd of over twenty-eight thousand.[13]

There were few Japanese accounts of Inouye's trials. Consistent with the growing sympathy for convicted war criminals, the accounts tended to emphasize the racism he encountered in his native Canada and the alienation from his ancestral home country. Moreover, later accounts point out that his conduct was not dissimilar from most camp guards and that he stood out only because he spoke such good English and was easily remembered by the POWs. Sumi Kojima wrote for a regional journal, *Nomin Bungaku* (Agricultural Literature), about *haka nashi bito* (people with no graves) concerning a young Canadian-born Japanese "whose life was cut short as a war criminal only because he was an interpreter for the Japanese."[14] In a postwar investigative report prepared by the Japanese government, Kanao Inouye is "presented as an admirable man"[15] who sang patriotic hymns as he went to his death.

For forty years after his execution, the case of Kanao Inouye was largely ignored. It was not until 1991 that the National Film Board's series *The Valour and the Horror*[16] brought his life back to public attention. Widely viewed in Canada and probably accepted by many as accurate, the documentary announced at its beginning that "this is a true story ... there is no fiction," even though what followed was largely fictional. Inouye was introduced with menacing music as a camp guard at Sham Shui Po and as "a member of the Japanese Gestapo, the Kempeitai." The narrator grimly reported that "at least two wounded Canadians died after beatings by Inouye," but no details or names were given to back up this allegation. The inaccuracies multiplied when the documentary described his postwar fate. The producers stated that Inouye was "found guilty of beating Canadian soldiers to death" and that his conviction was set aside as "Canada couldn't try a Canadian citizen for war crimes," both of which were not true. The only section of the documentary that is in any way accurate is a recollection from a surviving prisoner to whom Inouye introduced himself: "I want you to know that I was born and raised in Kamloops, British Columbia and that I hate your goddamn guts." Inouye went on to describe how when he was growing up, he had been called a "little yellow bastard" and now his tormentors would pay.

Over time, the notion of a sadistic Japanese prison guard emerging from the bland conformity of the British Columbia Interior captured media attention. He became a significant focus of nationalists who branded him as a repellent evil. In 2007, Canada's popular history journal the *Beaver Magazine* published an article on "Canada's Hall of Infamy," a compilation by historians of the greatest villains in Canada's past.[17] Kanao Inouye featured prominently on the list. He was, according to David Bercuson, the "leading death camp torturer."[18] He was certainly an irascible presence in the Canadian POW camp, which was by no means a death camp, nor was it clear that he was the worst of the staff. Bercuson also took a cavalier approach to the facts and misstated Inouye's birthdate and indicated that his treason trial took place in Canada.

The falsehoods and legends seemed to build up over time. In a bombastic piece published in the *Toronto Sun* in 2018, titled "Kamloops Kid: Treason Treated with a Rope," the newspaper gave a wildly inaccurate portrayal of Inouye.[19] According to the *Sun*, "Canadian, British and Chinese soldiers testified he was responsible for the deaths of at least eight Canadian soldiers,"[20] an account that is utterly false. There was no such testimony and there was no proof of any deaths. Facts were simply tossed aside in the interests of inflammatory journalism to vilify this "proficient torturer and master of cruelty."[21] As late as 2021, the *Globe and Mail* would print a retrospective on "C" Force in which the often stated and never substantiated assertion that Inouye was responsible for "killing several vulnerable men" — the number of victims seemed to have a life of its own varying from two to eight — was yet again made.[22]

Beyond the bombast in the common press, serious reconsiderations of Inouye's life and fate began to emerge. A far more balanced look at Inouye, *Mutual Hostages: Canadians and Japanese During the Second World War*, was published in 1990. The authors referred at length to affidavits from POWs that established Inouye as a vengeful and violent figure in the camps. But they also stated that he was "responsible for several deaths and countless beatings," although this was never established in court proceedings.[23] After a time, there was even some sympathy for him. In 2015, the Toronto Fringe Festival featured a short play, *Interrogation: Lives and Times of the Kamloops Kid.* According to one of the performers the purpose was "to humanize him" and suggest that he did not act "out of malice." Another performer commented that "he was caught in between Canada and trying to prove his loyalty to Japan."[24]

Kanao Inouye's hanging was the last and likely the final time a Canadian would be executed for treason. This is not to say that there would not still be traitors. After the Gouzenko affair in 1945–46, several Canadians prominent in the military and government were revealed as Soviet spies. While the press called for treason charges, Canada was a recent ally of the U.S.S.R., and in any event, no state of war existed. As a result, Russian agents such as Montreal MP Fred Rose were prosecuted under the Official Secrets Act.[25] During the October Crisis of 1970, when Front de Libération du Québec terrorists captured a British consul and then a provincial minister, killing the latter, it could be argued that the insurgents attacked the foundation of the state. However, those apprehended were charged with kidnapping and murder instead of treason. There was no attempt to apply the treason provision in the Criminal Code, and several suspects were simply held for extended periods under the terms of the War Measures Act. Trying them for treason would likely have turned criminals into martyrs. Neither was treason invoked when police seized a terrorist, Hiva Mohammad Alizadeh, who imported bomb triggers into Canada in 2010. Instead, he was convicted under recently enacted anti-terrorism provisions. At Alizadeh's sentencing, Justice Colin McKinnon told him, "[you have] betrayed the trust of your government and your fellow citizens" and "you have effectively been convicted of treason."[26] But the reality was that the treason provisions were not invoked and were never likely to be used. They had become an outdated appendage waiting for their eventual repeal.

It would perhaps be easy to excuse Inouye's conduct by alleging that he himself was a victim of racism. This is a comfortable contemporary explanation, but it lacks any foundation in the actual proceedings. His war crimes trial was by no means a kangaroo court — it was a meticulous affair in which numerous witnesses attended and sworn affidavits were examined. Legal scholar Suzannah Linton's conclusion that the courts offered "a broadly fair trial in difficult circumstances"[27] is justified. If anything, Germans accused of war crimes seemed to have been judged on a higher standard. Those soldiers who were ordered to shoot escapees from the "Great Escape" were tried and executed. Their conduct was significantly less heinous than Niimori Genichiro's. There was considerable discontent among rank-and-file Allied staff that the Japanese were being granted unwarranted leniency. This might be due to the circumstances that the Western allies had endured: two harrowing world wars with Germany and a reckoning was at hand. The same feeling of traditional animosity did not exist toward Japan, and justice was tempered by an understanding that they would all have to co-exist in a postwar world.

•

As for the men who decided Kanao Inouye's fate, the postwar world was a comfortable one. After handling the Camp case of Tokunaga, Saito, and others, Puddicombe was tasked with even more significant trials. Three of the generals who led the Japanese invasion would be tried for the atrocities committed under their command. Puddicombe was entrusted with two of them. The first was against Maj. Gen. Shoji Toshishige, who commanded the 230th Regiment. His regiment fought against the West Brigade, which included many Winnipeg Grenadiers. After December 19, when their positions were overrun, several Canadians were killed without provocation and those who were wounded and unable to march to the prisoner compound were bayoneted by guards. Though the atrocities were well documented, survivors rarely had any way of identifying the troops involved. Shoji's lawyer suggested that the killers could well have come from other units, and he was acquitted.

The next trial concerned Maj. Gen. Tanaka Ryosaburo of the 229th Regiment. Puddicombe spent a great deal of time in preparation, and on one exercise, he walked the former battlefield accompanied by the accused. This time, Puddicombe was able to use maps and documents from the period to establish the location of the 229th. A witness swore that at the Salesian Mission, soldiers of the 229th deliberately bayoneted all of the male medical staff and told a Canadian officer who was spared for interrogation that eventually he too would be executed. For his failure to control his men, Tanaka was convicted and sentenced to twenty years imprisonment. As historian Mark Sweeney concluded, "There was a steep learning curve for Puddicombe in the courtroom,"[28] and while he had limited information for the Shoji trial, at the Tanaka trial he changed his approach and focused on finding evidence and witnesses that placed Tanaka's troops at the site of the atrocities. As a result, his efforts were rewarded with a conviction.

After completing these difficult trials with the limited resources available, Puddicombe received little recognition. By May 1947, the month after Inouye's final conviction, he had had enough and was ready to return to Canada. He reminded Orr that he had a family back in Canada. As well, he became disenchanted with the process and particularly its leadership: "I am afraid that their [British senior officers] attitude is they couldn't care less.... The Colonel 'A' here, has less than no interest in war crimes and his G.O.C. no more. It is looked on as a scruffy show from top to bottom, and I am closer to the bottom than the top."[29]

By September 1947, Puddicombe was back in Montreal and out of the army. No longer constrained by military discipline from speaking his mind, he gave the press plenty to report on regarding the Far East war crimes trials. What especially infuriated him was the outcome of the Camp trial of Tokunaga, Saito, and others. He recounted to a reporter from the *Montreal Standard* how Tokunaga ordered the execution without trial of four Canadian escapees and that Saito's indifference to the diphtheria outbreak led to the deaths of one hundred others. He asked, "How many men does a man have to kill to be hanged?"[30] Frequently called on to speak to business or veterans' groups, Puddicombe kept a stock speech in which his finale was a condemnation of the senior British military. The Tokunaga-Saito case was heard by an experienced military court that considered all the evidence and many witnesses over a period of fifty-four days. The reviewing officer accepted the findings of fact, but for unknown reasons revoked the death penalty. There was no indication that the reviewing officer was legally trained or competent. It was apparent that after more than a year, Puddicombe was still seething: "I am prepared to maintain that these commutations were more the result of ignorant and arrogant stupidity, unwarranted and definitely harmful in their effect."[31] As for the Inouye case, Puddicombe had little to add other than a mild gloat: "He [Inouye] had assisted in a number of interrogations, which is a Japanese euphemism for torturing, some of his victims had undoubtedly died. It is satisfying to report that Inouye Kanao, alias Kamloops Kid, alias Slap Happy has gone to join his more, or less, honourable ancestors."[32]

Before he left Japan, Lt. Col. Oscar Orr was given an unexpected assignment. With several thousand Japanese Canadians being repatriated, Ottawa felt that there should be some organization to receive them. Orr became the liaison for Canada's Department of Labour in charge of getting the repatriates on their feet in war-torn Japan. It was a task completely at odds with his job of prosecuting war criminals, but Orr took to it. In August 1946, he described his work in bringing the repatriates ashore and getting them accommodation and financial support. He saw to it that those who were ill received treatment, and he advised Ottawa that the only hospital "would hardly rate as a first-class slum by Canadian standards."[33] Orr developed sympathy for the Japanese Canadians, and in a report at the end of 1946, he pleaded with Ottawa for further aid. He frequently talked or wrote about the hard life of the repatriates. He conceded that what happened to them was beyond his mandate, but many of them were still Canadian citizens and Canada should do what it could to help the repatriates. Orr could at least draw some satisfaction that he had done what he could and was awarded the Member of the Order of the British Empire in 1947 to recognize outstanding noncombat military service. In 1953, he left law practice and became a police magistrate, serving until 1962. After a long and fruitful life, he died at age one hundred in 1992.

Orr's efforts to assist the repatriates was one element in the King government's postwar strategy toward Japanese Canadians. In a February 1946 ruling, the Supreme Court of Canada gave conditional approval to the deportation policy but denied that forced deportation could be applied to Canadian-born citizens or dependents. For three years after the end of the war, those Japanese Canadians who resettled in the Prairies or in Ontario could not return to the Pacific coast. Martha Inouye and her family were fortunate, as their neighbours in B.C. preserved their belongings and returned them after the war. Thereafter, they moved to Toronto and simply got on with life: "Now we're kind of scattered throughout Canada, wherever we wanted to go ... you're not living in a close community like we used to."[34] But for many others, there was little reason to return to B.C., for their property and livelihoods were confiscated with inadequate or no compensation. It was not until 1949 that Japanese Canadians were even allowed to vote. The mistreatment of an entire group of people based on their ethnicity became the subject of continual reflection in Canada, aided by powerful accounts of the trauma of the relocations and internment such as Joy Kogawa's *Obasan*. Finally, in 1988, then prime minister Brian Mulroney issued a formal apology on behalf of Canadians for the wartime hysteria, and limited compensation was provided to those who had been deprived of so much.

The survivors of Sham Shui Po and the Japanese labour camps were liberated by the end of August 1945 and made their way back to Canada by September. The prolonged malnutrition and mistreatment took a toll and many had a hard time adjusting to civilian life and resuming family ties. Others would spend the rest of their lives dealing with blindness or paralysis resulting from their time in the camps. One survivor, Dr. Ken Cambon, felt that "the experience left you feeling life in so many different colors."[35] He would go to medical school and live every day of the rest of his life to the fullest. R.T. Johnson of the Winnipeg Grenadiers was given a medical clearance and then told to forget about his experiences. But he could not: "Now after 60 years it still haunts me. It plays over and over in my head like a real life horror movie."[36] The years of near-starvation and grinding labour had profound effects and left the survivors subject to illness and shortened life spans. Capt. John Norris, who had endured Inouye's parade ground beating, returned to Winnipeg. He was a broken man and required hospitalization; the years of prolonged malnutrition left their mark, and it was months before he could return to the family's tailor shop. Shortly after the war, he was instrumental in establishing the Hong Kong Veterans Association. One survivor felt that Norris never recovered from his ordeal in December 1942, and he became "a quiet, slow-moving figure limping along with a cane for the rest of his time."[37] John Norris died in 1949 at the age of forty-four.

In 1951, the Canadian government paid the survivors a dollar for each day of confinement. Eight years later, they added an additional fifty cents. In 1966, a return to Hong Kong was organized by the Hong Kong Veterans Association. Many of the veterans found the city unrecognizable. Sham Shui Po camp was eventually demolished and turned into a park in 1993. At least one reminder would be built in Canada. In 2009, the Hong Kong Memorial Wall naming all 1,976 men of "C" Force was dedicated in Ottawa. With carved mountains atop the memorial, the topography of Hong Kong was reproduced as a reminder of where the men served and died.[38]

As for the surviving victims of torture, Mary Power remained in Hong Kong until 1957. That year, she retired to England and died in 1967. The White Australia policy was sufficiently relaxed to enable Albert Guest and his family to settle in that country. As for John Power's trio of informants, the "Three Musketeers," upon their release in 1944 they continued to pass on intelligence to Allied agents. Mohammed Hassan was again arrested and spent the rest of the war in jail. Much like John Norris, Ahmed Khan never recovered from his torture sessions and died shortly after the end of the war.

Other survivors also simply could not adjust. Sgt. Arthur Rance of the Hong Kong Volunteers, who took the initial steps to identify Inouye and greatly assisted the Canadian prosecutions in Japan, became increasingly erratic after the end of the war. He stole an expensive coat from one of the Canadian officers and thereafter ran up a huge bill at the Peninsula Hotel, which he had no intention of paying. "I felt his character was unstable," Puddicombe concluded.[39]

During the war, Tse Dickuan devoted himself to transcribing the nominal rolls of the prisoners and smuggling them out of the camps, which allowed the Allies to gain insight into the status of prisoners who were still alive. He even worked in the office of the military commander Tokunaga and was able to smuggle information on Japanese activities out to the Allies. Tse was a precious source of up-to-date information on the POWs and their fate until November 1944, when he fled Hong Kong, fearing that he would be uncovered. He kept contact with a Miss Ho Chun Ye, still in Hong Kong, who maintained communications with the prisoners but later disappeared and was likely killed by the Japanese before the end of the war. The devotion of agents such Tse and Miss Ho was a tribute to the courage of Hong Kong citizens in resisting the occupation, and they were priceless sources of information for Puddicombe on the course of mistreatment and lack of medical attention given to the prisoners. After the war, Tse was awarded the British Empire Medal.[40]

In June 1946, Puddicombe discovered that Rev. Watanabe Kiyoshi was living on charity in Kowloon. There was little left for him in Japan, for his wife and daughter had died in the Hiroshima blast. Puddicombe was aware that Watanabe was instrumental in smuggling serum into the Bowen Road Hospital at the height of the diphtheria epidemic, and he believed that "the Dominion of Canada owes Watanabe a deep depth of gratitude."[41] A few months later, Watanabe was brought back to Japan and despite his limitations with the language, was hired on as an interpreter in Tokyo. Veterans of the Royal Rifles heard about his plight and put together a collection of one hundred dollars for him.

Pursuant to prison policy, Inouye's body was buried on Stanley Prison grounds. In Kanagawa Prefecture, Japan, his name was eventually inscribed on the Inouye family headstone. In 1970, one of his sister Martha's daughters visited Japan with her father for the Osaka Expo '70 and paid their respects at the memorial for Tadashi and Kanao in Atsugi.

ACKNOWLEDGEMENTS

RESEARCH ON A TOPIC THAT OCCURRED IN THE PAST OVER AN EX-tended area required the help of several persons and institutions that I would like to thank. Vito Chiu of the Public Records Office of Hong Kong was of great assistance finding records on the Inouye case and making them available. Rebecca Murray assisted me with the holdings of Library and Archives Canada, while Suzanne Lemaire of the same institution helped with reproductions. Kira Baker of the Vancouver City Archives assisted with background on the Inouye family and schooling. The staff of the Windsor Public Library, including Mae Whaley, Tom Vajdik, and Mary Lou Gellisen were most patient and of great assistance. Ms. Christine Seki was most generous in assisting with further information and observations, and her contributions are greatly appreciated.

I would especially like to thank Dr. Yuki Takatori, formerly of Georgia State University. Dr. Takatori was a mine of information with regard to Japanese names and background information. As well, she provided invaluable information from Japanese sources which helped provide a balanced view of these events.

Appendix

CHARGE SHEET

First Charge COMMITTING A WAR CRIME,
    in that he,
at Hong Kong, on or about the twenty first day of
December 1942, when an interpreter on the Prisoner
of War Camp Staff at Sham Shuipo Camp, in violation of the laws and usages of war, did assault Capt J.A.
NORRIS of the Winnipeg Grenadiers, Canadian Army
by beating him in full view of the Canadian prisoners of
war whilst they were drawn up on parade.

Second Charge COMMITTING A WAR CRIME,
    in that he,
at Hong Kong, on or about the twenty first day of
December 1942, when an interpreter on the Prisoner of
War staff at Shamshuipo camp in violation of the laws
and usages of war did assault Major F.T. ATKINSON,
Royal Rifles of Canada, Canadian Army by kicking him
in full view of the Canadian Prisoners of War whilst
they were drawn up on parade.

Third Charge COMMITTING A WAR CRIME,

in that he,

at Hong Kong between the 15th day of June and the 30th day of November 1944 when a member of the staff of the Japanese Gendarmerie Headquarters, in violation of the laws and usages of war, was concerned in the ill-treatment of civilian residents of Hong Kong under arrest at 67-69 Kimberley Road, Stanley Gaol and other places, resulting in the death of Mr. Power, Ip Kam Wing, So Shing Hon and Enrique Lee, in physical sufferings to others of the said persons and in particular to Mrs. M.V. Power, Mr. R.P. Ghilote, Dr. V.N. Atienza, Mr. A.E.P. Guest, Mr. A. Madar, Mr. G. Sang, Mr. W. Lawrence, Mohd Yousif Khan, Lai Chak Po, Lam Sik and Wong Sui Poy.

NOTES

1: Arrival

1   While the Japanese convention is to use the family name before the given name, Inouye followed the Western practice of given name first. He regularly spelled his name in this fashion.

2   Patricia E. Roy, *A White Man's Province: British Columbia Politicians and Chinese and Japanese Immigrants, 1858–1914*, (Vancouver: University of British Columbia Press, 1989), 92. The author cites 11,272 Japanese arrivals at Canadian ports between July 1, 1899, and August 30, 1900; however, many may have moved on to the US.

3   Roy, *A White Man's Province*, 117.

4   Roy, *A White Man's Province*, 207–9.

5   Laurier to Grey, December 5, 1907, MG 27 IIB2, Grey Papers, Library and Archives Canada (LAC); as quoted in Patricia E. Roy, J.L. Granatstein, Masako Iino, and Hiroko Takamura, *Mutual Hostages: Canadians and Japanese during the Second World War* (Toronto: University of Toronto Press, 1990), 11; on the Royal Commission on Chinese and Japanese Immigration, see Patricia E. Roy, *A White Man's Province: British Columbia Politicians and Chinese and Japanese Immigration, 1858–1914* (Vancouver: UBC Press, 1989), 109. Nothing in this introductory chapter is intended to be original or controversial; see also Ken Adachi, *The Enemy That Never Was: A History of the Japanese Canadians* (Toronto: McClelland and Stewart, 1976), chap. 1.

6 Roy, *A White Man's Province*, 177.

7 "Inland Capital," *Kamloops Standard*, April 4, 1908.

8 Adachi, *The Enemy That Never Was*, 40.

9 *Kamloops Standard*, October 22, 1908, quoting a report in the (Victoria) British Colonist.

10 See *Kamloops Standard*, May 7, 1912 — Ah Tom accused of running an opium joint in Kamloops.

11 *Kamloops Standard*, May 14, 1912; and on the fears of further Japanese immigration, see "Another Jap Invasion," editorial, *Kamloops Standard*, October 29, 1908.

12 Details on Mikuma Asada's origins are from Exhibit A, British Columbia Certificate of Birth, in Inouye trial, as well as from an Inouye interrogation by Hong Kong Special Branch in October 1945; details of the marriage are contained in Exhibit F, abstract from census record, file 13/2331/46, "War Criminals Inouye Kanao," Public Records Office, Hong Kong (PRO, HK), where Mikuma's name is indicated as being "Tamari."

13 My thanks to Prof. Yuki Takatori formerly of Georgia State University for explaining the significance of the name Kanao.

14 Adachi, *The Enemy That Never Was*, 102.

15 "Expect to Mobilize Full Company of Japs Within Thirty Days," *Vancouver Sun*, January 5, 1916.

16 Adachi, *The Enemy That Never Was*, 102–3.

17 All of the information on his military service is from the LAC, RG 150, Personnel Records of the First World War.

18 While the original citation has been lost and does not form part of his military record, it appears that Tow gave a copy to friends in Japan and that it was eventually published in a local booklet, "Hometown Heroes of Kanagawa Prefecture." See Iida Takashi, *Sagama jinkokki: Atsugi no rekishi o irodotta hyakunin* (Shimin Kawarabansha, 2000), Yale University Library; thanks to Prof. Yuki Takatori for bringing this to my attention.

19 As above, it is the LAC document.

20 Personnel Records of the First World War, Tow Inouye, Regimental Number 688274, RG 150, LAC.

21 On Tow Inouye in Maple Ridge, see Census of Canada, 1921, British Columbia, District 16. Ottawa, Dominion Bureau of Statistics.

22 The quote is Adachi at p. 149.

23 Patricia E. Roy, *The Oriental Question: Consolidating a White Man's Province*, (Vancouver: UBC Press, 2003), 41.

24 "Jimmie Robinson on Repatriation," *Merritt Herald*, April 4, 1919.

25 Canada, *House of Commons Debates*, June 15, 1920 (Colonel Peck).

26 See Exhibit F, abstract of census register, file 13/2331/46, Treason Trial, 1947, PRO, HK.

27 "The Vantech," Easter 1935, LH 3.V35 T32, City of Vancouver Archives.

28 Annexes A, B, and C, file 8767-40-C, vol. 3824, RG 25, LAC. There are several obfuscations and downright falsifications contained in Kanao Inouye's statements of his past. Several times he claimed that Inouye Tokutaro was his mother's father. His mother's family name was Asada. At his postwar briefing, he stated that he completed high school and left Canada in 1936 and thereafter went to Waseda University. However, that would have made him twenty years old and still in high school, an unusually advanced age. In both of his trials, he swore that he left school in 1935 and went to Japan in that year. That testimony agrees with Exhibit C, which was a confidential record of his past he prepared for his own use and provided at his civil trial. That exhibit shows him leaving Canada in June 1935 and a year later (as required by Japanese law) taking his preliminary tests for army service. It appears that he did attend Waseda Kokusai Gakuin, a prep school, for a brief period from 1936 until his call up for military service in March 1937. See Inouye testimony, p. 14, and Exhibit C, file 13/2331/46, "Inouye Trial," PRO, HK.

29 See Marius B. Jansen, *The Making of Modern Japan* (Cambridge: Belknap Press, 2000), 568–75; and Takafusa Nakamura and Konosuke Odaka, eds., *Economic History of Japan, 1914–1955: A Dual Structure*, trans. Noah Brannen (New York: Oxford University Press, 2003).

30 On the February 1936 coup attempt and the rising control of the militarists, see Andrew Gordon, *A Modern History of Japan: From Tokugawa Times to the Present* (New York: Oxford University Press, 2003), 196–203.

31 Rana Mitter, *Forgotten Ally: China's World War II, 1937–1945* (Boston: Houghton Mifflin Harcourt, 2013), 84.

32 The account of Inouye's life in the 1920s and 1930s is taken from his testimony at the court martial. This collection is a project of the Hong Kong University Libraries Digital Initiatives and provides scholarly access to forty-six of the war crimes files, held by the National Archives of the United Kingdom. See Hong Kong's War Crimes Trials Collection: Accused–Inouye, Kanao: Case No. WO/235/927 (hereafter cited as Inouye War Crimes Trial); see examination in chief, 80–81, and cross-examination, 102–8.

33 Kanao Inouye, quoted in Inouye War Crimes Trial, 81. Not all Nisei felt so out of place in Japan. Mary Tomita, who left the United States for Japan in

1939, recalled, "My memories of the pre-war years, when I was adjusting to a new culture and quite free to do as I pleased, are generally happy ones." "Coming of Age in Japan" *Amerasia Journal* 23, no. 1 (1997): 165–80.

34   Hong Kong War Crimes Collection, WO/235/927, Inouye's cross-examination at p. 108.

2: Sham Shui Po

1   On the battle for Hong Kong, see Brereton Greenhous, *"C" Force to Hong Kong: A Canadian Catastrophe, 1941–1945*, Canadian War Museum Publication No. 30 (Toronto: Dundurn Press, 1997); Tony Banham, *Not the Slightest Chance: The Defense of Hong Kong, 1941* (Vancouver: UBC Press, 2003); and Ted Ferguson, *Desperate Siege: The Battle of Hong Kong* (Toronto: Doubleday Canada, 1980).

2   Charles G. Roland, *Long Night's Journey into Day: Prisoners of War in Hong Kong and Japan, 1941–1945* (Waterloo, ON: Wilfrid Laurier University Press, 2001) 48; Charles G. Roland, "Massacre and Rape in Hong Kong: Two Case Studies Involving Medical Personnel and Patients," *Journal of Contemporary History* 32, no. 1 (1997): 52–61.

3   Quoted in Jonathan F. Vance, *Objects of Concern: Canadian Prisoners of War Through the Twentieth Century* (Vancouver, UBC Press, 1994), 186.

4   Daniel G. Dancocks, *In Enemy Hands: Canadian Prisoners of War, 1939–45* (Edmonton: Hurtig, 1983), 236–37; see Roland, *Long Night's Journey*, 162, and chap. 6 for a full account of the prisoners' hospital: "On November 11, 1942, there were 301 Canadians in hospital, being cared for by the four medical officers and 40 medical orderlies (almost all untrained volunteers)" (166).

5   *Parliamentary Debates*, Commons, (March 10, 1942), vol. 378, 930.

6   "No Reprisals," *New Canadian* (Vancouver), March 12, 1942, 2.

7   Ann Gomer Sunahara, *The Politics of Racism: The Uprooting of Japanese Canadians During the Second World War* (Toronto: J. Lorimer), 29.

8   On the observations of Frank Power, see Exhibit G, affidavit of Frank Gavan Power, sworn January 31, 1946, Inouye Court Martial.

9   Meirion and Susie Harries, *Soldiers of the Sun: The Rise and Fall of the Imperial Japanese Army* (New York: Random House, 1991), 482.

10   B. Griess, ed., *The Second World War: Asia and the Pacific* (Wayne, NJ: U.S.M.A. West Point, 2002), 8. On Mizuki, see Robert Citino, "Fire for Effect: Toughing It Out in the Japanese Army," historynet.com; on the beating of American POWs, see Gavan Daws, *Prisoners of the Japanese: POWs of World War II in the Pacific* (New York: William Morrow, 1994), 101–6.

11 Examination-in-chief. Inouye War Crimes Trial, 82.

12 See Norris's description in Exhibit I, affidavit of John A. Norris, September 26, 1942, Inouye Court Martial.

13 William Allister, *Where Life and Death Hold Hands* (Toronto: Stoddart, 1989), 80; Allister's account is questionable. He describes the beating of Captain Norris by Inouye as being the result of Norris having told Red Cross officials that a camp inspection was a set-up and that the prisoners were being beaten and underfed. This is clearly refuted by Norris's own account of what happened on the parade ground in December 1942.

14 Allister, 80.

15 Allister, 80.

16 Allister, 81.

17 Liam Nolan, *Small Man of Nanataki: The True Story of a Japanese Who Risked His Life to Provide Comfort for His Enemies* (New York: Dutton, 1966), 28–30.

18 Nolan, *Small Man of Nanataki*, 28–30.

19 Dancocks, *In Enemy Hands*, 240.

20 Dancocks, *In Enemy Hands*, 240.

21 Sergeant Lance Ross, quoted in *The Royal Rifles of Canada in Hong Kong 1941–1945* (Carp, ON: The Hong Kong Veterans Commemorative Association, 2001), 294.

22 Corbett, quoted in Dancocks, *In Enemy Hands*, 240–1; on Lt. Frank Power's comments on the beating of Chaplain Green, see Exhibit G, Inouye Court Martial, affidavit of Frank Gavan Power, as well as Victor Ebbage, *The Hard Way: Surviving Shamshuipo POW Camp* (Cheltenham, UK: History Press, 2011), 163.

23 Examination-in-chief, Inouye War Crimes Trial, 85.

3: Kempeitai

1 The authorities took considerable interest in Ho Wai Ming, and she was the subject of two reports, one by the British military and the other by Hong Kong Special Branch police: see Annexures C and D, file 8767-40-C, vol. 3824, RG 25, LAC.

2 Inouye War Crimes Trial, 86; on being hired by the Kempeitai, see *China Mail*, April 17, 1947, report of trial proceedings April 16, 1947.

3 *China Mail*, April 17, 1947; on Sgt. Maj. Hayashi Sadatoro's comments, see Accused Noma Kennosuke, file WO 235/999, 408, Hong Kong's War Crimes Trial Collection.

4   Philip Snow, *The Fall of Hong Kong: Britain, China and the Japanese Occupation* (New Haven: Yale University Press, 2003), 80–84; on the Indians in Hong Kong, see Jenny Chan and Derek Pua, *Three Years Eight Months: The Forgotten Struggle of Hong Kong's WWII* (n.p.: Pacific Atrocities Education, 2019).

5   Roland, *Long Night's Journey*, 313.

6   Examination of James Anderson, Inouye War Crimes Trial, 72; for comments from the former gendarme, see Roland, *Long Night's Journey*, 313.

7   Raymond Lamont-Brown, *Kempeitai: Japan's Dreaded Secret Police* (Gloucestershire, UK: Sutton, 1998), 11.

8   Hong Kong Trials Collection, trial of Noma Kennosuke, January–February 1947, testimony of Hayashi Sadataro, p. 408.

9   Hong Kong Trials Collection, trial of Noma Kennosuke, January–February 1947, testimony of Hayashi Sadataro, p. 408.

10   Shiozawa testimony at the treason trial p. 4.

11   *China Mail*, September 11, 1945.

12   September 22, 1945.

13   *China Mail*, October 29, 1945.

14   *China Mail*, October 29, 1945.

15   Suzannah Linton, "Rediscovering the War Crimes Trials in Hong Kong, 1946–48," *Melbourne Journal of International Law* 13, (2012): 291.

16   Snow, *Fall of Hong Kong*, 308.

17   Memo from Marcel Cadieux, External Affairs, "Punishment of War Criminals," based on a memorandum from Paul Tremblay, April 15, 1943, 626-40C, file 2, vol. 2, 108, RG 25, LAC.

18   On pronouncements limiting Canadian participation to crimes against its servicemen, see HQS 8959-9-5: Hopkins to Secretary CWCAC, June 5, 1945, vol. 2906, RG 24, LAC.

19   John Read, "Note for the Prime Minister," June 12, 1945, vol. 4, St. Laurent Papers, MG 26L, LAC.

20   Patrick Brode, *Casual Slaughters and Accidental Judgments: Canadian War Crimes Prosecutions, 1944–1948* (Toronto: Osgoode Society/University of Toronto Press, 1977).

21   Affidavit of James Riley, attached to part of the Paul Tremblay report to Read, January 14, 1944, part 1, file 5908-40, vol. 3247, RG 25, LAC.

22   "Recipes Favorite Topic of Hong Kong Prisoners," *Globe and Mail*, October 12, 1945.

23   "Canucks Left Tied in Snow," *Toronto Star*, September 13, 1945.

24 "Work Until You Die," *Toronto Star*, September 14, 1945.

25 "Tom Forsyth," in Hong Kong Veterans Commemorative Association, hkvca.ca/historical/accounts/forsyth/forsyth.php; on the returning prisoners' affidavits, see report from Paul Matthews, Deputy Minister Army to Under-Secretary of State for External Affairs, April 4, 1946, file 8767-40C, vol. 3824, RG 25, LAC.

26 LAC, RG 25, vol. 3824, file 8767-40C, affidavit of Edwin Barlow, sworn December 12, 1945; affidavit of Frank Jiggins, sworn February 21, 1946; affidavit of Frank Gavin Power, sworn January 11, 1946.

4: Arrest

1 Peter MacRitchie, "B.C. Jap Was Nippon Spy Most Cruel to Canadians," *Toronto Star*, September 11, 1945.

2 Peter MacRitchie, "B.C. Jap Was Nippon Spy Most Cruel to Canadians," *Toronto Star*, September 11, 1945.

3 "First Reports Tell of Jap Camp Life," *Vancouver Sun*, September 15, 1945.

4 "First Reports Tell of Jap Camp Life," *Vancouver Sun*, September 15, 1945; "Prisoner Tormented by Jap from Canada," *Winnipeg Free Press*, September 11, 1945.

5 House of Commons Debates, September 14, 1945, 177.

6 "Notes from Interrogation of Inouye Kanao by Major A.N. Carstairs on December 16, 1945," file 8767-40C, vol. 3824, RG 25, LAC.

7 "Notes from Interrogation of Inouye Kanao by Major A.N. Carstairs on December 16, 1945," file 8767-40C, vol. 3824, RG 25, LAC.

8 Sergeant Arthur Rance, quoted in P.G.R. Campbell to External Affairs, September 18, 1945, file 8767-40C, vol. 3824, RG 25, LAC (hereafter cited as Inouye File).

9 Sergeant Arthur Rance, quoted in P.G.R. Campbell to External Affairs, September 18, 1945, file 8767-40C, vol. 3824, RG 25, LAC.

10 LAC 25, RG 25, vol. 3824, report of P.R.G. Campbell to External Affairs, September 18, 1945.

11 Patricia E. Roy, *The Triumph of Citizenship: The Japanese and Chinese in Canada, 1941–67* (Vancouver: UBC Press, 2007), 49.

12 University of Victoria, Landscapes of Injustice series, 3.13, Ian Mackenzie nomination speech, September 18, 1944.

13 Sunahara, *The Politics of Racism*, 31 and 116.

14 Courtesy Inouye family, Interview with Martha Yano, 1 November 1995, Toronto, p. 53.

15 LAC 25 RG 25, vol. 3824 report of P.G.R. Campbell to External Affairs, September 18, 1945.

16 *New Canadian*, September 19, 1945.

17 *New Canadian*, September 19, 1945.

18 Report of C.M.A. Strathy and R.D. Jennings to War Crimes Advisory Committee November 30, 1945, file 5908-40, part 5, vol. 3728, RG 25, LAC.

19 On the American proposal that Canadians participate in the prosecutions, see Acting Secretary of State for External Affairs to High Commissioner, November 6, 1945, file 4060-13-40-C, vol. 3641, 25, LAC. On the Canadian agreement to participate, see Cabinet Conclusions, January 16, 1946, vol. 419, MG 26-J4, LAC. On the extraordinary meeting of the War Crimes Advisory Committee, see Minutes dated September 21, 1945, file 4060-13-40-C, vol. 3641, 25, LAC.

20 A detailed account of the formation and deployment of the War Crimes Liaison Detachment–Far East is given in Mark Sweeney, "The Canadian War Crimes Liaison Detachment–Far East and the Prosecution of Japanese "Minor" War Crimes," (PhD diss., University of Western Ontario, 2013); sketch of Oscar Orr at Sweeney, 42.

21 Orr memorandum, December 22, 1945, file 4060-C-40 part 1, vol. 3641, RG 25, LAC.

22 "Unmerited Mercy," Montreal *Standard*, October 4, 1947.

23 On Puddicombe's career, see an obituary notice by Jean-Jacques Lefebvre, "Nos disparus: George Beverley Puddicombe," *La revue de barreau* 31 (January 1972): 69–70.

24 File 2.31, Puddicombe fonds, MG 30, LAC, MG 30. The stock speech prepared by Puddicombe and left among his papers contains his description of his arrival in Hong Kong and the British investigations.

25 LAC, Puddicombe fonds, MG 30, E 567, file 2.1, Notes for a speech to the Celanese Company, Montreal, March 2, 1948.

26 LAC, Puddicombe fonds, MG 30, E 567, file 2.1, Notes for a speech to the Celanese Company, Montreal, March 2, 1948.

5: Political Football

1 On the mass identification parade, see the trial of George Wong, in *China Mail*, April 17, 1946.

2 *China Mail*, April 17, 1946.

3 *China Mail*, April 17, 1946.

4 *China Mail*, April 17, 1946.

5   *China Mail*, April 17, 1946.
6   *China Mail*, April 17, 1946.
7   *China Mail*, April 17, 1946.
8   Inouye examination at the trial of George Wong, *China Mail*, April 17, 1946; on George Wong, see Snow, *Fall of Hong Kong*, 127.
9   Inouye examination at the trial of George Wong, *China Mail*, April 17, 1946; on George Wong, see Snow, *Fall of Hong Kong*, 127.
10 A masterful explanation of the legal basis for the British military trials is provided in Suzannah Linton, "Rediscovering the War Crimes Trials in Hong Kong, 1946–48," at 293–97.
11 Inouye file, Campbell Deputy Minister to External Affairs, February 19, 1946.
12 Inouye file, Campbell Deputy Minister to External Affairs, February 19, 1946.
13 Inouye file, Norman Robertson to Deputy Minister of Justice, March 2, 1946.
14 Campbell, Deputy Minister (Army) to External Affairs, February 19, 1946, Inouye File; Norman Robertson, External Affairs to Deputy Minister of Justice, March 2, 1946; F.P. Varcoe, Justice to External Affairs, March 9, 1946, Inouye File.
15 Inouye file, E.R. Hopkins to Secretary of State for External Affairs, March 22, 1946; note of approval by Norman Robertson.
16 E.R. Hopkins to Secretary of State for External Affairs, May 15, 1946, Inouye File; on the previous correspondence regarding what to do with Inouye, see E.R. Hopkins, March 22, 1946, Inouye File; B. Campbell to Justice, April 12, 1946, Inouye File; F.P. Varcoe to External Affairs, May 10, 1946, Inouye File.
17 Inouye file, Hopkins to External Affairs, May 15, 1946.
18 Memorandum from Minister of Justice and Attorney General of Canada, May 24, 1946, Inouye file.

6: Godown Justice
1   Memorandum (undated), file 2.30, Puddicombe fonds, MG 30, LAC.
2   Memorandum (undated), file 2.30, Puddicombe fonds, MG 30, LAC.
3   Exhibit I, affidavit of John A. Norris, Inouye Court Martial.
4   Throughout the trial transcript, the commandant is referred to as "Sakaino." In Canadian affidavits, his name is spelled as "Sakoina"; when Inouye requested his presence as a witness, he requested "Lt. Saikano."
5   Exhibit I, affidavit of John A. Norris, Inouye Court Martial.

6   Exhibit I, John A. Norris, Inouye Court Martial; Exhibit J, F.T. Atkinson, Inouye Court Martial; Exhibit G, Frank Gavan Power, Inouye Court Martial.

7   Exhibit G, affidavit of Frank Gavan Power, Inouye Court Martial.

8   Notes for speech at the Canadian Celanese Company, March 2, 1948, file 2.31, E 567, Puddicombe fonds, MG 30, LAC.

9   Puddicombe summation, Inouye Court Martial, 138.

10   Examination of Lam Sik, Inouye Court Martial, 5.

11   Examination of Lam Sik, Inouye Court Martial, 6.

12   Hong Kong War Crimes Trials Collection, WO/235/927, trial of Kanao Inouye, p. 16.

13   Examination-in-chief of Rampal Ghilote, Inouye Court Martial, 17.

14   Examination-in-chief of Rampal Ghilote, Inouye Court Martial, 18.

15   Examination-in-chief of Rampal Ghilote, Inouye Court Martial, 18.

16   Snow, *Fall of Hong Kong*, 181. An extended description of the British Army Aid Group and its activities is included on pp. 177–87.

17   Examination-in-chief of Rampal Ghilote, Inouye Court Martial, 18.

18   Exhibit O, affidavit of Mohamed Yousif Khan, dated September 27, 1945, Inouye Court Martial.

19   Ex Parte Quirin, 317 U.S. 1 (1942).

20   Cross-examination of Rampal Ghilote, Inouye Court Martial, 21–27.

21   Cross-examination of Rampal Ghilote, Inouye Court Martial, 27.

22   Examination-in-chief of Mary Power, Inouye Court Martial, 10.

23   Memorandum (undated), file 2.30, Puddicombe fonds, MG 30, LAC.

24   Examination of Mary Power, Inouye Court Martial, 12.

25   Examination of Mary Power, Inouye Court Martial, 14.

26   Examination of Rampal Ghilote, Inouye Court Martial, 20.

27   Cross-examination of Rampal Ghilote, Inouye Court Martial, 26.

28   Examination-in-chief of A. Madar, Inouye Court Martial, 30.

29   Puddicombe summation, Inouye Court Martial, 139.

30   Puddicombe summation, Inouye Court Martial, 140; and examination of Arthur Guest, Inouye Court Martial, 60–62.

31   Examination-in-chief of Arthur Guest, Inouye Court Martial, 60.

7: Only Obeying Orders

1   Examination of Kanao Inouye, Inouye War Crimes Trial, 81.

2   Examination of Kanao Inouye, Inouye War Crimes Trial, 81.

3   Roland, *Long Night's Journey*, 49.

4 Examination-in-chief of Kanao Inouye, Inouye War Crimes Trial, 84.

5 Examination-in-chief of Kanao Inouye, Inouye War Crimes Trial, 84.

6 Examination of Kanao Inouye, Inouye War Crimes Trial, 85.

7 Cross-examination of Kanao Inouye, Inouye War Crimes Trial, 112.

8 Examination by the court of Kanao Inouye, Inouye War Crimes Trial, 130–31.

9 Examination-in-chief of Kanao Inouye, Inouye War Crimes Trial, 91–92.

10 Examination of Kanao Inouye, Inouye War Crimes Trial, 101.

11 Examination-in-chief of Kanao Inouye, Inouye War Crimes Trial, 101.

12 Roy Ito, *Stories of My People* (Hamilton, ON: Nisei Veterans Association, 1994), 357; a briefer version of his encounter with Inouye is contained in his book *We Went to War* (Stittsville: Canada's Wings, 1984), 269–72.

13 Cross-examination of Kanao Inouye, Inouye War Crimes Trial, 102.

14 Cross-examination of Kanao Inouye, Inouye War Crimes Trial, 122 and 125.

15 Cross-examination of Kanao Inouye, Inouye War Crimes Trial, 128.

16 Cross-examination of Kanao Inouye, Inouye War Crimes Trial, 128.

17 Re-examination of Kanao Inouye, Inouye War Crimes Trial, 130–33.

18 Puddicombe summation, Inouye War Crimes Trial, 142.

19 Puddicombe summation, Inouye War Crimes Trial, 142.

20 J.R. Pritchard, "Lessons from British Proceedings Against Japanese War Criminals," *Human Rights Review* 3 (1978): 109.

21 Haggan summation, Inouye War Crimes Trial, 143.

22 Haggan summation, Inouye War Crimes Trial, 145.

23 Haggan summation, Inouye War Crimes Trial, 147.

24 Haggan summation, Inouye War Crimes Trial, 148.

25 Verdict, Inouye War Crimes Trial, 149. Pritchard, "Lessons from British Proceedings Against Japanese War Criminals," 119. Pritchard notes that another interpreter in North Borneo was given the same punishment for mistreating prisoners.

26 Pritchard, "Lessons from British Proceedings Against Japanese War Criminals," 119. Pritchard notes that another interpreter in North Borneo was given the same punishment for mistreating prisoners.

8: Decision Annulled

1 "'Slap Happy Joe' to Die," *Kamloops Sentinel*, May 29, 1946.

2 "'Slap Happy Joe' to Die," *Kamloops Sentinel*, May 29, 1946.

3 "BC Born Jap Must Die for Atrocities," *Vancouver Sun*, May 26, 1946.

4 Roy et al., *Mutual Hostages*, 185.

5 "All Japanese Ordered Out of BC: East of the Rockies or Back to Japan," *Vancouver Sun*, March 16, 1945.

6 Mona Oikawa, interview of Martha Inouye, November 1, 1995.

7 "All Japanese Ordered Out of BC," *Vancouver Sun*, March 16, 1945.

8 Sunahara, *The Politics of Racism*, 138; on the family separation, see *Toronto Star*, May 27, 1946.

9 Ito, *Stories of My People*, 358.

10 Ito, *Stories of My People*, 358.

11 Lutz Oette, "From Calculated Cruelty to Casual Violence – The United Nations War Crimes Commission and the Prosecution of Torture and Ill Treatment," (2014) Crim. Law Forum, 25, 302.

12 Petition dated June 6, 1946, 2–4, WO/235/927, trial of Kanao Inouye, May 1946, Hong Kong's War Crimes Trial Collection.

13 Testimony of Hayashi Sadataro, 408, WO 235/999, trial of Noma Kennosuke, February 1947, Hong Kong's War Crimes Trial Collection.

14 Puddicombe to Orr, July 9, 1946, Inouye File.

15 A thorough and compelling account of the Niimori Genichiro case is contained in Mark Sweeney, "The Canadian War Crimes Liaison Detachment–Far East and the Prosecution of Japanese 'Minor' War Crimes," (PhD diss., University of Waterloo, 2013), 154–61.

16 Mark Sweeney, "The Canadian War Crimes Liaison Detachment–Far East and the Prosecution of Japanese 'Minor' War Crimes," (PhD diss., University of Waterloo, 2013), 154–61.

17 *China Mail*, December 4, 1946.

18 Private Barnett, quoted in "Appalling Conditions," *China Mail*, December 6, 1946.

19 Sweeney, "The Canadian War Crimes Liaison Detachment," 125, see *China Mail*, January 30, 1947.

20 "Appalling Conditions," *China Mail*, December 6, 1946; "Stodda an Example of a Sneak," *China Mail*, December 7, 1946.

21 Sweeney, "The Canadian War Crimes Liaison Detachment," 153.

22 Montreal *Standard*, October 4, 1947.

23 Inouye file, Puddicombe to Orr, July 9, 1946.

24 Puddicombe to Orr, July 9, 1946, Inouye File; Orr to Puddicombe September 4, 1946, Inouye File.

25 Kerin to O.C. Land Forces, Hong Kong, November 14, 1946, Inouye File.

9: Treason?

1   Deputy Minister Ross to External Affairs, November 6, 1946, Inouye File; and see Orr's message to Secretary, Department of National Defence, October 14, 1946, Inouye File; the reply from External Affairs in Wershof to Department of National Defence (Army) November 8, 1946, Inouye File.

2   Puddicombe fonds, LAC, MG 30, Orr to Puddicombe, October 29, 1946.

3   Puddicombe to Orr, November 8, 1946, Inouye File; Norman to Gascoigne, November 13, 1946; see also Orr to Puddicombe, October 29, 1946, file 1.28, MG 30, Puddicombe fonds, LAC.

4   E.H. Norman to External Affairs, November 25, 1946, Inouye File; and Gascoigne to Norman, November 21, 1946, Inouye File.

5   Puddicombe fonds, MG 30, Lonsdale to Puddicombe, February 1, 1947.

6   Orr to Puddicombe, December 5, 1946, Inouye File.

7   Orr to Puddicombe, December 5, 1946, Inouye File.

8   Orr to Puddicombe, December 5, 1946, Inouye File.

9   Orr to Puddicombe, December 5, 1946, Inouye File.

10 Orr to Puddicombe, December 5, 1946, Inouye File.

11 Orr to Puddicombe, December 5, 1946, Inouye File.

12 Orr to Secretary, Department of National Defence, December 12, 1946, Inouye File.

13 Puddicombe to Orr, February 10, 1947, file 2.9, Puddicombe fonds, MG 30, LAC.

14 Deputy Minister Army to Justice, December 9, 1946, Inouye File; External Affairs to Justice, December 11, 1946, Inouye File; F.P. Varcoe, Justice to External Affairs, December 13, 1946, Inouye File.

15 Hong Kong War Crimes Trials Collection, WO 235/999, trial of Noma Kennosuke, January 9, 1947, p. 283.

16 See "High Treason," *South China Morning Post*, February 27, 1947; "Treason Trial," *South China Morning Post*, February 28, 1947; "Inouye for Trial," *South China Morning Post*, March 1, 1947.

17 Treason Act 1351, 25 Edw. 3, St. 5, c. 2.

18 Patrick Brode, *Sir John Beverley Robinson: Bone and Sinew of the Compact* (Toronto: Osgoode Society/University of Toronto Press, 1984), 23–25.

19 Philip Girard, Jim Phillips, and R. Blake Brown, *A History of Law in Canada: Beginnings to 1866*, vol. 1 (Toronto: Osgoode Society/University of Toronto Press, 2018), 510.

20 T. Flanagan, *Louis "David" Riel: Prophet of the New World* (Toronto, 1979); and Lewis H. Thomas, "Louis Riel," in *Dictionary of Canadian Biography*, vol. 11 (Toronto: University of Toronto Press, 1982), 736–52.

21 H.L. Wessling, "Robert Brasillach and the Temptation of Fascism" in *Certain Ideas and France: Essays on French History and Civilization* (Westport, CT: Greenwood Press, 2002) 67–74.

22 Evan Kindley, "The Insanity Defence: Coming to Trems with Ezra Pound's Politics," *The Nation* (April 2018).

23 Francis Selwyn, *Hitler's Englishman: The Crime of Lord Haw-Haw* (London: Routledge, 1987). On the legal issues, see W.H. Lawrence, "Rex v. Lord Haw-Haw," *Hastings Law Journal* 73 (1950).

24 Inouye file, Puddicombe to Orr, July 9, 1946.

10: Defence Gamble

1 Ito, *Stories of My People*, 365.

2 Puddicombe to Orr, February 10, 1947, file 2.9, Puddicombe fonds, MG 30, LAC.

3 Item 26 (a memorandum recording the major comments made during the trial, which is not a transcript of a verbatim account), file 13/2331/46 "War Criminals Inouye Kanao" (hereafter cited as Treason Trial).

4 Treason Trial, 4.

5 Treason Trial, 5.

6 Treason Trial; "Loseby states that after consulting with his client, he is not disputing that accused adhered to and aided and comforted the King's enemies," 6.

7 "Hung Up and Burned … Woman's Face Burned," *South China Morning Post*, April 18, 1947.

8 Treason Trial, 7.

9 Treason Trial, 8.

10 Snow, *Fall of Hong Kong*, 212; on the 1943 repression see 185–87.

11 A full account of Khan's testimony is given in "The Three Musketeers," *China Mail*, April 18, 1947.

12 Treason Trial, 12.

13 Treason Trial, 13.

14 Treason Trial, 9.

15 Pritchard, "Lessons from British Proceedings Against Japanese War Criminals," 110. Several other witnesses, Wong King Cheun and Wong Yau

Sang, likewise had no connection to the BAAG but were nevertheless beaten by Inouye at Stanley Prison.

16   Treason Trial, 14.
17   Treason Trial, 10.

11: Exhibit C

1   Treason Trial, 14.
2   Treason Trial, 14.
3   Treason Trial, 15.
4   *China Mail*, April 18, 1947.
5   "Nisei in His Imperial Majesty's Service," mansell.com and Carey McWilliams, "The Nisei in Japan," *Far Eastern Survey* 13, (1944): 70.
6   Treason Trial, 15.
7   Treason Trial, 15.
8   Treason Trial, 15.
9   Treason Trial, 15.
10 *South China Morning Post*, April 22, 1947.
11 *China Mail*, April 19, 1947.
12 Treason Trial, 15.
13 *China Mail*, April 19, 1947.
14 *China Mail*, April 19, 1947.
15 This incident is not mentioned in the memorandum of the trial but is reported in *China Mail*, April 19, 1947.
16 Treason Trial, 16.
17 *China Mail*, April 19, 1947.
18 Treason Trial, 16.
19 *South China Morning Post*, April 19, 1947.
20 See Kawashima Yasuhide, *The Tokyo Rose Case: Treason on Trial* (Lawrence: University Press of Kansas, 2013). Iva D'Aquino's conviction was questioned on the basis that the jury never heard any broadcasts and that prosecution witnesses had been coached to present a warped view of her conduct. She was eventually pardoned in 1977.
21 Treason Trial, 18.
22 Cécile Fabre, "The Morality of Treason," *Law and Philosophy* 39, (2020): 427–61.
23 *China Mail*, April 23, 1947.
24 *China Mail*, April 23, 1947.
25 *China Mail*, April 23, 1947.

26 "Judge's Summing Up," Treason Trial, 17.
27 *R v. Ahlers*, (1915) 1 King's Bench 616 at 625.
28 "Judge's Summing Up," Treason Trial, 7–8.
29 Judge's summation, 17.
30 *China Mail*, April 23, 1947.

12: Technicalities of Law

1   "Petition of Kanao Inouye," April 24, 1947, file 13/2331/46, PRO, HK.
2   "Petition of Kanao Inouye," April 24, 1947, file 13/2331/46, PRO, HK.
3   Documents noted as received by Captain J.R. Haggan, May 8, 1947, "Petition of Kanao Inouye," April 24, 1947, file 13/2331/46, PRO, HK.
4   *China Mail*, May 28, 1947.
5   *China Mail*, May 28, 1947.
6   "Housing Problem," *China Mail*, July 11, 1947.
7   "Letter to the editor," *China Mail*, August 2, 1947.
8   *China Mail*, July 2, 1947; and see *Inouye v. The King, International Law Report*, vol. 14.
9   As discussed in *China Mail*, July 17, 1947; and see *Joyce v. DPP* (1946) Appeal Cases 347.
10 *China Mail*, July 2, 1947.
11 *China Mail*, July 2, 1947.
12 *China Mail*, July 17, 1947.
13 *China Mail*, July 17, 1947.
14 Report of the Chief Justice, July 22, 1947, 13/2331/46, PRO, HK.
15 Report of the Chief Justice, July 22, 1947, 13/2331/46, PRO, HK.
16 "Graphic Story of Ordeal," *China Mail*, July 11, 1947.
17 Lt. Col. Read Collins, UK Liaison Mission Tokyo to Land Forces Hong Kong, July 22, 1947, 13/2331/46, PRO, HK.
18 M.H. Harrison to Haggan, July 28, 1947, 13/2331/46, PRO, HK.
19 Governor of Hong Kong to Secretary of State for the Colonies, August 2, 1947, 13/2331/46, PRO, HK; and see Sir Henry Blackall's note on the oral judgment of the Court, August 11, 1947; "Warrant for Carrying out Sentence of Death," issued by Colonial Secretary, August 19, 1947, 13/2331/46, PRO, HK.
20 Petition of Kanao Inouye August 15, 1947, 13/2331/46, PRO, HK.
21 Affidavit of Kanao Inouye and attachments, August 15, 1947, 13/2331/46, PRO, HK.
22 "Warrant for Carrying Out Sentence of Death, *Rex v. Inouye Kanao*, August 19, 1947, 13/2331/46, PRO, HK.

23 Petition of Kanao Inouye, August 20, 1947, PRO, HK.
24 Petition of Kanao Inouye, August 20, 1947, PRO, HK.
25 Kayoko Takeda, *Interpreters and War Crimes* (London: Routledge, 2021), 93: with thanks to Prof. Yuki Takatori for this reference.

13: End of a Scruffy Show

1 The Convention on Certain Questions Relating to the Conflict of Nationality Laws, The Hague, April 12, 1930, third paragraph of preamble; and see David A. Martin, "Dual Nationality: T.R.'s 'Self-Evident Absurdity'" (Chair Lecure, October 27, 2004 in *UVA Lawyer*, (Spring 2005), "Theodore Roosevelt Weighs In," para 3.
2 Orr to SCAP General Headquarters, December 5, 1945, Inouye File. On the question of dual citizenship, see Ilan Zvi Baron, "The Problem of Dual Loyalty," *Canadian Journal of Political Science* 42, no. 4 (2009): 1025–44.
3 Lyman Poore Duff, *Royal Commission to Inquire into and Report upon the Organization, Authorization and Dispatch of the Canadian Expeditionary Force to the Crown Colony of Hong Kong*, (Ottawa: King's Printer, 1942).
4 Carl Vincent, *No Reason Why* (Stittsville, ON: Canada's Wings, 1981); but see Terry Copp, "The Decision to Reinforce Hong Kong: September 1941," *Canadian Military History* 20 (2011): 3–13, which recounts the diplomatic and military situation as of September 1941 and finds that there were persuasive reasons why the force might be dispatched.
5 "Canadian-Born Jap Hanged in Hong Kong," *Toronto Star*, August 26, 1947; *New Canadian* (Vancouver), September 6, 1947.
6 "Canadian-Born Jap Hanged in Hong Kong," *Toronto Star*, August 26, 1947; *New Canadian* (Vancouver), September 6, 1947.
7 Inouye File, J.E. Duggan, Registrar of Canadian Citizenship to External Affairs, June 2, 1949.
8 Reginald Allen, "The Trial of Socrates: A Study in the Morality of the Criminal Process," in Martin Friedland, ed., *Courts and Trials: A Multidisciplinary Approach* (Toronto: University of Toronto Press, 1975), 4, 10.
9 Pritchard, "Lessons from British proceedings Against Japanese War Criminals," 119. He notes that another interpreter in North Borneo was given the same punishment for mistreating prisoners.
10 John W. Dower, *Embracing Defeat: Japan in the Wake of World War II* (New York: W.W. Norton, 1999), 508.
11 Urs Matthias Zachman, "Loser's Justice: The Tokyo Trial from the Perspective of the Japanese Defence Counsels and the Legal Community," in

Kerstin von Lingen, ed., *Transcultural Justice at the Tokyo Tribunal* (Leiden, Netherlands: Brill, 2018), 301.

12 Michael Lucken, *The Japanese and the War: From Expectation to Memory* (New York: Columbia University Press, 2013), xvii.

13 Dower, *Embracing Defeat*, 515.

14 Sumi Kojima, "Canadian Immigrants, Their Glory and Tragedy," in *Nomin Bungaku* (Agricultural Literature), cited in Iida Takashi, *Sagami jinkokki: Atsugi, Aiko no rekishi o irodotta hyakunin* (Hometown Heroes of Kanagawa Prefecture), (Atsugi-shi: Shimin Kawarabansha, 2000). Many thanks to Prof. Takatori for locating this.

15 Kayoko Takeda, *Interpreters and War Crimes* (New York: Routledge, 2021), 93.

16 "Savage Christmas: Hong Kong, 1941," *The Valour and the Horror*, directed by Brian McKenna, script by Terence and Brian McKenna (Ottawa: National Film Board of Canada, 1991).

17 David Bercuson et al., "Canada's Hall of Infamy," *Beaver Magazine* (2007): 87.

18 David Bercuson et al., "Canada's Hall of Infamy," *Beaver Magazine* (2007): 87.

19 Brad Hunter, "Kamloops Kid: Treason Treated with a Rope," *Toronto Sun*, November 4, 2018.

20 *Toronto Sun*, November 4, 2018.

21 *Toronto Sun*, November 4, 2018.

22 Tim Cook, "The Three Battles of Canada's Hong Kong Veterans," *Globe and Mail*, December 17, 2021. The Inouye case is an amazing example of camp rumours becoming accepted as history. Surviving POWs interviewed upon their return to Canada frequently commented on how Inouye had murdered some of their comrades. However, Canadian legal officers concluded that there was no such evidence and he was never charged at either of his trials with killing a POW. Nevertheless, the rumours had a life of their own and by dint of repetition became accepted as fact. Just to give an example, in Tim Cook's 2020 book *The Fight for History: 75 Years of Forgetting, Remembering, and Remaking Canada's Second World War* (Toronto: Allen Lane) the author repeats as fact the gossip that Inouye "sadistically beat, humiliated, and killed several Canadians at the camps" (274–75).

In the same vein, POW gossip had it that Captain John Norris was beaten by Inouye for protesting the theft of Red Cross parcels. This is stated as fact in William Allister, *Where Life and Death Hold Hands* (Toronto: Stoddart,

1989) 81–83 and repeated in Jonathon F. Vance's *Objects of Concern: Canadian Prisoners of War Through the Twentieth Century* (Vancouver: UBC Press, 1994) 188. It is clearly a fiction, for several eye-witness affidavits, including Norris's own account state that the beating was a consequence of the missing troops and had no relation to Red Cross parcels.

23 Roy et al., *Mutual Hostages*, x.

24 Quoted in *Nikkei Voice* (Toronto), June 25, 2015.

25 On Fred Rose and the Gouzenko Affair, see Amy Knight, *How the Cold War Began: The Gouzenko Affair and the Hunt for Soviet Spies* (Toronto: McClelland & Stewart, 2005), 126–27.

26 "Hiva Alizadeh Pleads Guilty to Terror Plot," *Ottawa Citizen*, September 18, 2014.

27 Suzannah Linton, ed., *Hong Kong's War Crimes Trials* (Oxford: Oxford University Press, 2013), 61.

28 Sweeney, "The Canadian War Crimes Liaison Detachment," 123; chap. 3 is a compelling account of both the Shoji and Tanaka trials.

29 Puddicombe to Orr, May 14, 1947, file 2.9, Puddicombe fonds, MG 30, LAC.

30 Puddicombe, quoted in "Unmerited Mercy," *Montreal Standard*, October 4, 1947.

31 Notes for speech at the Canadian Celanese Company, March 2, 1948, file 2.31, E 567, Puddicombe fonds, MG 30, LAC.

32 Notes for speech at the Canadian Celanese Company, March 2, 1948, file 2.31. E 567, Puddicombe fonds, MG 30, LAC.

33 Oscar Orr to Department of National Defence, December 17, 1946, file 23-2-17, vol. 660, RG 27, *Landscapes of Injustice*, University of Victoria Archives.

34 Martha Inouye, interview by family, November 1, 1995. Courtesy of Christine Seki.

35 Ken Cambon, interview with Dr. Charles Roland, June 10, 1983, Charles G. Roland fonds, McMaster University.

36 On R.T. Johnson, see "Individual Report: H6192 Richard Johnson," Hong Kong Veterans Commemorative Association, hkvca.ca/cforcedata/indivreport/indivdetailed.php?regtno=H6192.

37 Quoted in Allister, *Where Life and Death Hold Hands*, 83.

38 Alexandra McKinnon, "The Battle of Hong Kong, Forgotten and Remembered: C Force, Cultural Memory and Commemoration," *Canadian Military History* 30, no. 2 (2021).

39 On Watanabe Kiyoshi, see Puddicombe to Orr, June 12, 1946, and Orr to Puddicombe, January 9, 1947, file 2.19, Puddicombe fonds, MG 30,

LAC; on Arthur Rance, see Puddicombe to Orr, February 10, 1947, file 2.9, Puddicombe fonds, MG 30, LAC.

40   Gwulo: Old Hong Kong, gwulo.com/comment/30861, Dickuan, Tse, BAAG No. 76iii, (undated).

41   LAC, Puddicombe fonds, MG 30, file 2.19, Puddicombe to Orr, June 12, 1946.

IMAGE CREDITS

11 Courtesy of Inouye family.

18 Unknown photographer. Department of National Defence, Library and Archives Canada, PA-114891.

29 PO Jack Hawes. Department of National Defence, Library and Archives Canada, PA-139015.

43 Unknown photographer. Library and Archives Canada, George B. Puddicombe fonds, 5706000.

56 Unknown photographer. Library and Archives Canada, George B. Puddicombe fonds, 5705999.

62 Unknown photographer. Library and Archives Canada, George B. Puddicombe fonds, 3817004.

113 Hedda Morrison. Harvard-Yenching Library, HM.C71D Box 2. Reproduced by permission from Harvard-Yenching Library.

INDEX

References to Kanao Inouye indicated by "KI."

Adachi, Ken, 9
Adams River Lumber Company, 7–8
Ahlers Case, 132–33, 139–40
ALFSEA (Allied Land Forces South
    East Asia), 40, 104–5
  quashes conviction, 91, 96, 102
Alizadeh, Hira Mohammed, 152
Allister, William, 22
Atienza, Vincente (doctor), 66–67, 69,
    78, 116, 114, 161–62
Australia, 38, 62, 68, 96, 128, 157

BAAG (British Army Aid Group),
    43–44, 62–64, 84, 117–19
Beaver Magazine, 151
Bercuson, David, 151
Blackall, Sir Henry, 111, 114, 124–27,
    146
  reports KI case, 139–40
  summing up, 130–34
Bowen Road Hospital, 19, 93, 158
Brasillach, Robert, 108

British Columbia, 5–15, 156
  anti-Japanese sentiment in, 10–11,
    20, 88

"C" Force, 17–19, 22, 32, 147, 151–57
Cambon, Ken (doctor), 156
"Camp case," 92–95, 112, 153
Campbell, Basil, 51
Campbell, P.G.R., 36
Canadian Army, 5, 8–10,
  in Hong Kong, 17–19, 147–48
Canadian War Crimes Liaison
    Detachment–Far East, 40–42, 91, 114
Carstairs, A.M., 36
China Mail, 30, 120, 130, 136
Chinese Canadians, 5–7
Chung Chuck v. The King (1930), 142
Clague, Douglas, 63, 117
Corbett, Claude, 24
Cousens, Charles, 128–29
Crawford, John (doctor), 19, 58–59

da Silva, M.A., 48–49
D'Aquino, Iva. *See* Tokyo Rose
diphtheria, 19, 21, 24, 57–58, 93–94,
    154, 158
Doucett (rifleman), 92
dual nationality. *See* nationality issue
Duff, Lyman Poore, 147

Eden, Anthony, 19–20
espionage, 62–64, 74, 75
    Japanese procedures, 118–19
External Affairs, Department of (Canada)
    disinterest in war crimes, 31–38
    and KI's case, 51–52, 99–101 104,
        148

Fulton, E.D., 36

Gascoigne, Alvary, 100–101
Gaudin, Ken (corporal), 19
Geneva Convention (1929), 39, 64
Ghilote, Rampal, 47, 49, 74–75, 78, 90
    at treason trial, 90, 115–16
    at war crimes trial, 60–62, 64–69
Globe and Mail (Toronto), 151
Gould (judge), 139–40
Green, Eric (Roman Catholic chaplain),
    24, 48
Guest, Albert, 75, 79, 127, 157
    at treason trial, 118–19
    at war crimes trial, 68–69

Haggan, John Reeves, 59, 89–90,
    112–14, 124–25, 141
    background, 56
    conducts KI's defence, 64–69,
        71–85, 148
Hague Convention (1930), 39, 146
Hassan, Mohammed (Assan Khan),
    117, 157
Hayashi, Sadatoro, 28, 91
Ho Wai Ming, 25–26, 28, 87
Hogg, Arthur (Major), 42, *43*, 44, 56

Hong Kong, 14, 20, 18–19, 28–30,
    48–53, 60, 158
    atrocities in, 26, 100
    battle of, 18–19, 147–48
    Indians in, 17, 27, 61, 63, 117
    post-war, 29–30, 137
Hong Kong Memorial Wall, 157
Hong Kong Veterans Association,
    156–57
Hongkong Telegraph, 102
Hopkins, E.R., 52

Inouye, Kanao, 22–24, 28, 32–33, 41,
    47–53, 91, 146–49
    appeal treason conviction, 135–40
    arrested, 35–36
    birth and youth, 8, 12
    Canadian indecision over, 51–56
    conflicting stories on background,
        77, 122–24, 145–46, 165n28
    execution, 1–3, 142–43
    goes to Japan, 13–19
    petition (1946), 87–91, 96–97
    rumours about, 151, 180n22
    treason charges, 102–3, 105
    treason trial, 111–34
    war crimes trial, 55–65, 72–85
Inouye, Martha, 8, *11*, 12, 37–38, 88, 152
Inouye, Mikuma, 8, *11*, 12–13, 38, 102
Inouye, Tokutaro, 13, 14, 36, 76
    background, *11*, 12
Inouye, Tow (Tadashi), 12, 102, 158
    background, 5–6
    military service, 8–10
Inouye family, 8, *11*
international law, 31, 81
    and Canada, 31–32, 40–42
    and Japan, 39
    KI's case in, 146–47
    Potsdam Proclamation (1945), 50
    See also Geneva Convention (1929);
        Hague Convention (1930); war
        crimes

INDEX

Interrogation: Lives and Times of the Kamloops Kid (play), 152
Ip, Kam-Wing, 68
Ito, Roy, 76–77, 89, 112
Iwai & Company, 24, 26

Japan, 5, 6, 9, 11, 12–14, 25
  and Geneva Convention (1925), 39
  post-war, 149–50
Japanese Army, 17, 26, 122, 123
  attacks Hong Kong, 18–19
  discipline of, 21, 83
  KI in, 122–24
Japanese Canadian War Memorial, 10, 37
Japanese Canadians 5–7, 8–9
  deportation of, 37, 87–89, 155–56
  racism against, 10–11
Jardine Matheson's East Point Godown, 55
Jiggins, Frank, 32–33
Joyce, William (Lord "Haw-Haw"), 108–9, 113, 136, 138
Justice, Department of (Canada), 51
  disapproves action against KI, 104

Kamloops, British Columbia, 7–11, 35–36, 90, 114, 133, 150
Kamloops Sentinel, 87
Kamloops Standard, 7
Kanagawa Prefecture, 5, 8, 12, 158
Kaul, B.N., 56, 92
Keio Electric Railway Company, 11–12, 13
Kempeitai, 14, 49, 50, 63, 73–75, 101, 115, 127
  crackdowns, 117
  methods, 26–28, 118–19
Kerin, F.C.A. (colonel), 96
Khan, Ahmed, 64, 117, 157
Khan, Mohamed Yousif, 63–64, 117–18
King, William Lyon Mackenzie, 31, 32, 36, 51, 89, 99, 147, 155
Koa Kikan, 48

Lai Chak Po, 68, 71, 119
Lam Sik, 60, 63, 89
Landau, Aaron, 141
Lawson, J.K. (brigadier), 18
  See also Canadian Army
Lee, Enrique, 47, 118
  See also war crimes
Lo Hin Shing, 49–50
Loie, David, 63, 117
Lonsdale, A., 102, 104, 106
  conducts prosecution, 111–34
Loseby, Charles, 111
  appeal, 135–42
  defends KI, 113–35

MacRitchie, Peter. *See* Inouye, Kanao
Madar, Ame, 67, 71, 119
Matsuda, Kenichiro, 26, 115
Montreal Standard, 95, 154
Moriyama (sergeant), 28, 60–64, 73–78, 79, 80, 118, 120, 142
Mutual Hostages: Canadians and Japanese During the Second World War, 151–52

National Defence, Department of, (Canada), 99, 104
nationality issue, 90–91, 105, 114, 125–26
  considered at treason trial, 128–29, 131–33
  dual nationality, 129, 140, 146, 148
  Orr's opinion, 102–3
New Canadian, 20, 37, 38, 148
Niigata POW Camp, 32, 42
Niimori, Genichiro, 44, 91–92
Nisei (foreign-born Japanese), 37, 88, 123, 126
  status in Japan, 14, 71–72
Nishi (interpreter), 75, 80
No Reason Why (Vincent), 147
Nogami, Fred, 76, 89
Noma, Kennosuke, 27, 61, 67, 105

Norman, E.H., 100–105, 148
Norris, John, 22, 33, 41, 72–73, 82–83
  affidavit at war crimes trial, 56–59
  post-war, 156

Obasan, 156
Oette, Lutz, 90
Ormsby, M.I., 56, 92
Orr, Oscar, 91–96, 154
  career, 40–44
  post-war, 155
  suggests treason trial, 99–100, 102–4

Peninsula Hotel, 60, 74, 115, 157
Popoff internment camp, 38
Power, Frank, 24, 33, 95
  affidavit of, 59
Power, John, 61–67, 75, 115, 117, 157
Power, Mary, 48–49, 61, 73–74, 79, 83,
  116, 171, 157
  at war crimes trial, 65–67
Prisoners of War (Canadian), 19–23,
  36–37
  survivors, 156–57
Pritchard, R.J., 82
  See also war crimes
Puddicombe, George, 44–45, 55,
  91–96, 100, 114
  background, 42–43
  conducts war crimes trial, 57–85
  post-war, 153–55

Rance, Arthur, 36–37, 96, 103, 157
Read, John, 31
Red Cross, 19, 24, 26, 93
Ride, Lindsay, 62
Riley, James (private), 32
Robertson, Norman, 51–52
Rogers (brigadier), 95
Ross, Lance, 23–24
Royal Commission on Chinese and
  Japanese Immigration, Session
  1902, 5

Royal Rifles of Canada, 17–19, 23, 32,
  42, 158
Royal Warrant (1945), 50

Sai Wan cemetery, 137
Sainsbury (magistrate), 100, 103
Saito Shunkichi (doctor), 19, 154
  war crimes trial, 92–95, 112
Sakaino (lieutenant), 58–59, 72–73, 80
Sang, Gonzalo, 47, 68–69, 75, 78, 89
Sequiera, Felizerto, 118
Sham Shui Po POW camp, 17, 19–21,
  22, 29, 58, 91, 93, 156
Shiozawa, Kunio, 26, 28, 116
Shoji, Toshishige, 153
69 Kimberley Road, 48, 60, 61, 65, 69,
  112, 115, 140
South China Morning Post, 95, 116, 125
South East Asia Command, 30
Stanley Prison, 1, 47, 64, 67, 73, 76, 89,
  91, 116, 158
Stewart, J.C. (colonel), 55–56, 67,
  79–81, 92
  sentencing of KI, 83–84, 90, 149
Stodda. *See* Tsutada, Itsuo
Sumi, Kojima, 150
Sunahara, Ann, 20
Supreme Court of Canada, 88, 155
Supreme Court of Hong Kong, 112–13,
  113, 116–17
Sweeney, Mark, 95, 154

Tanaka, Ryosaburo, 153–54
Tokunaga, Isao, 22, 24, 26, 44, 72, 112,
  150, 154
  trial of, 92–95
Tokyo Rose, 128–29
Tokyo Trial, 149
Toronto Star, 88, 148
Toronto Sun, 151
Treachery Act (1940), 51–52, 91
treason, 49, 50, 51, 108, 113, 128–29
  in Canadian law, 100–101, 106–7, 152

Treason Act (1351), 49, 51
  defined, 106
treason trial, KI's, 111–32
Trist, George, 59
Tse, Dickuan, 44, 157–58
Tsutada, Itsuo, 33, 104, 112, 149
  trial of, 94–95

United Kingdom, 28, 30–31, 38
United States, 23, 40 48, 64, 128

Valour and the Horror (NFB series), 150
Vancouver, 6, 8, 10, 12, *18*, 37, 40,
  76–77, 88
Vancouver Sun, 8, 36, 87–88
Vancouver Technical High School,
  12–13
Varcoe, F.P., 51, 104
Vincent, Carl, 147

war crimes, 18–20, 32, 27–28
  Canada policy, 31
  against Chinese, 24, 116–17
  KI war crimes trial, 55–85
  other trials, 91–95, 153–54
  against POWS, 14–15, 30
  torture, 82, 90
War Crimes Investigation Section for
  Asia, 39–40
Waseda Kokisai Gakuin (prep school),
  14, 78, 122
water torture, 14, 27, 47–49, 61, 64,
  68–69, 72–82, 115–19, 126
Wershof, M.H., 99–100
Williams (judge), 136, 139
Winnipeg Free Press, 36
Winnipeg Grenadiers, 17, 22, 24, 32,
  57, 153, 156
Wong, George, 65, 68, 79
  trial of, 47–50
Wong Pui, 116
Woo, H.K. (solicitor), 111–12, 135

Yamashita precedent, 81
Young, Sir Mark, 101, 105

ABOUT THE AUTHOR

Patrick Brode has written extensively on Canadian history and law. His works include a biography of one of Canada's early jurists, Chief Justice John Robinson, as well as *Courted and Abandoned*, a study of the tort of seduction on the frontier. His more recent writing includes *Death in the Queen City*, about the racially charged murder trial of Clara Ford in Toronto in 1895, *The Slasher Killings* on the anti-gay hysteria that accompanied a serial killing in Windsor in 1945, as well as a survey of Canada's investigation and prosecution of war crimes after the Second World War. Five of these works have been short-listed for Canadian book awards. Patrick was formerly a lecturer at the University of Windsor Faculty of Law. He lives in Windsor, Ontario, and has practiced law there since 1977.